DISCOVERING FINANCIAL FREEDOM

LEGACY
Press Books

Published by Legacy Press Books, an imprint of End Game Press
LegacyPressBooks.org
Your life tells a story; we can help you write it.

Terry Moore
4041 Marsh Lane
Carrollton, TX 75007
contact@advancedbiblicalfoundations.org

ISBN (print): 978-1-63797-157-4
ISBN (eBook): 978-1-63797-158-1

Edited by Misty Urban, www.madwriters.net
Cover and interior design and layout by Nelly Murariu @PixBeeDesign.com

ADVANCED FOUNDATIONS

Discovering Financial Freedom

Living in the Generosity of God

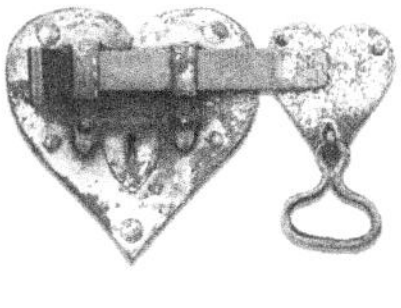

TERRY MOORE

CONTENTS

INTRODUCTION

We are living in a day and time when things are out of control in many ways, literally, and we truly need to understand what God's Word says about how we are to live our lives and walk in His ways. The Word of God is under attack and has been for a long time. However, the only real stability is found in the Bible and the truth therein that will make and keep us free.

The core of the Christian faith is in developing an intimate, personal relationship with Jesus Christ as Lord and Savior. I believe God really desires for us to know Him in a personal way—not simply to know more facts and stories about Him, but to really know Him. All healthy human relationships include effective communication, and our relationship with the Lord is no different. His longing is that we would take seriously His principles, directives, and leading so we would live a life built upon the Rock and so that the circumstances of life, the economy, lawlessness, or corruption would not shake our security or our peace.

Finances are one of those areas in which God wants to speak to us. Many people say that the church talks about money too much, but do you realize that there are 2,300 verses in the Bible that have to do with wealth, money, and finances? And Jesus talked about money in sixteen of His thirty-eight parables. That's a lot! Maybe we don't talk about it enough. Maybe Jesus knew this. He had plenty to say about it, as we shall see, because money is so intertwined in everything we do. How you handle money says volumes about your perspective on life and your priorities.

We have a government that's in enormous debt—approaching $30 trillion at this writing, not counting the government's other obligations. We have a financial system that's not being regulated and many think that the answer is to just print more money (a.k.a., the "modern monetary theory")!

At one time, I was caught up in this world's pursuit of wealth. I went to college to get a degree in business and took every finance course available. My goal—to become rich! And I chased that with gusto. I knew how to build a financial statement so I could borrow more money, operating on hundreds of thousands of dollars in lines of credit. I was chasing deals and making deals. Yes, I was making money, but I was also making a lot of debt. I really had never considered what the Word of God had to say about money, wealth, or riches. And then, in 1982, God changed my life.

As I studied the Word, I began to see that my wrong thinking and mindset were not according to God's ways. Painfully, I started to change the way I had been doing business and handling money. I sought the Lord for help. He heard. I was deeply in debt, but God intervened on many occasions with miracles that could not be explained. It took me eight years to pay off everything and get out of debt, but along the way, I learned valuable lessons and principles that solidly govern my life today.

Most of us have to work and earn money in order to live. Not everyone has the same kind of financial issues, but everyone has to deal with money, whether you have a lot or a little. It affects nearly every area of your life. That's why it's important to understand what God says about money.

Critical to financial freedom is the principle of *blessing*—that God wants to pour out blessings upon us, not just for our sake, but also because He wants our blessings to pour through us to others. "Blessed to be a blessing!" He is a good Father and provider, promising that He will meet "ALL your needs according to His riches in glory by Christ Jesus" (Philippians 4:19).

Yes, we will be impacted by the world in which we live, and there will be struggles. Unplanned expenses or needs may arise; unemployment, medical issues, car repairs, school tuition, and all of our possessions demand our time and resources. There may even be long seasons of drought when there just is not enough money left at the end of the month. However, God has laid out valuable principles in His Word to govern our decision-making and managing of finances to bring us through these hard times and into provision and peace.

His promise is, "These things I have spoken to you, that in Me you may have peace. In the world you will have tribulation; but be of good cheer, I have overcome the world" (John 16:33).

I invite you to join me in enjoying the abundant life and *Discovering Financial Freedom!*

Terry Moore

Founding Pastor and Elder, Sojourn Church Carrollton, TX
Founder and President of Advanced Biblical Foundations,
advancedbiblicalfoundations.org

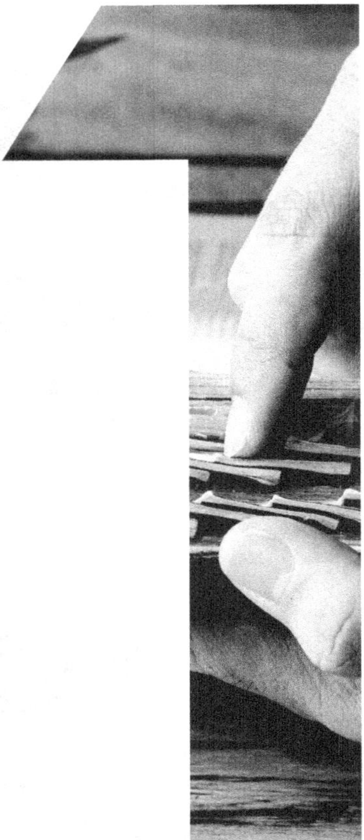

Getting God's Perspective

The earth is the Lord's and the fullness thereof.
Psalm 24:1

It is important that we start at the beginning. "*The earth is the Lord's and the fullness thereof.*" Everything begins here. It's a position and perspective that is critical to get us on the right track to financial freedom. Here's another interesting Scripture which ties into a foundational principle concerning finances: Haggai 2:8 says, "The silver is Mine and the gold is Mine, says the Lord of hosts." Let's be clear—everything belongs to God. It's all His. God spoke these words in Haggai 2:8 to encourage his servants to set their hands to the work before them and restore the Temple.

What is the message of this passage? When God speaks and states that the silver and gold are His, He is in fact proclaiming His sovereignty and title to the earth's resources as the Creator and Owner of all things. In Psalm 50:10, He also declares, "For every beast of the forest is mine, and the cattle upon a thousand hills." These verses make it clear that mortal man is not the true owner of the resources of this earth, contrary to what most believe. Truly, all things are held in the grace and hands of God.

God is both the ruler and owner of all the oil, sea, and earth resources. He owns the airspace and the galaxies, and not one iota of anything that was made was made without His ingenuity and workmanship (John 1:1-2).

Defining Stewardship

So what is our role, our position? We are *stewards*, not owners. What is a steward? It's a person who looks after and is responsible for the property of another. God has given us charge over all of His creation, but He wants us to carry out the responsibilities according to His instructions. He has told us what to do and how to manage His household and possessions. Let's look at the Scripture in Luke 16:10-13. This is the parable of the unjust steward:

> He who is faithful in what is least is faithful also in much; and he who is unjust in what is least is unjust also in much. Therefore if you have not been faithful in the unrighteous mammon, who will commit to your trust the true riches? And if you have not been faithful in what is another man's, who will give you what is your own?
>
> No servant can serve two masters; for either he will hate the one and love the other, or else he will be loyal to the one and despise the other. You cannot serve God and mammon.

In this story, it is obvious that the Master fully expected his steward to manage the financial affairs of his estate. But the steward was careless, fearful, and not faithful with what he had been given.

This foundational principle is paramount all throughout Scriptures and this study. We have to recognize that all things belong to God. We have the opportunity to steward and manage the resources He has given us, but we must learn how to submit to His Lordship and be faithful in our responsibilities. The Word says that if you are faithful in the least, you will be faithful in much. If you are faithful with another man's possessions, you will be given your own—you'll be given more.

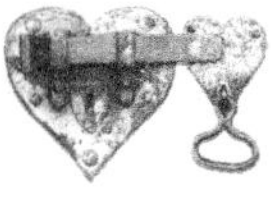

"God has given us stewardship over all His creation."

You've heard people say, "Well, if I had more, I could do more with it. If I had more money, I'd be okay or making better decisions." No, that's not what the Word says. It says, if you're not faithful with what you have now, you won't be faithful with greater things. I've said the same thing—I need more! The widow woman in the New Testament (Luke 21:1-4) didn't have much either, yet she gave it all away and was honored because of that.

Perhaps you have been looking at the subject of finances from the wrong perspective—like looking through a pair of binoculars from the wrong end. If so, it's time to turn things around. Instead of asking for more, make a commitment to steward what you already have and be faithful in the little—in whatever God has given to you.

In verse 11, Luke 16 says, "Therefore if you have not been faithful in the unrighteous mammon, who will commit to your trust the true riches?"

It's clear that faithfulness is the key point in these verses. Being faithful suggests that you are trustworthy. It's not that complicated. You assume responsibility for what God gives to you. But you manage those things according to His rules, His instructions—you don't do whatever you want to do. You are a steward of God's resources.

The Love of Money

The book of Luke addresses this issue of loyalty and commitment and servanthood. "No servant can serve two masters; for either he will hate the one and love the other, or else he will be loyal to the one and despise the other. You cannot serve God and mammon" (Luke 16:13). There's that word "mammon" again. This word literally refers to a deity, although it more commonly refers in a negative context to something that is at odds with service to God. It carries with it a spiritual content as well.

This verse says that you will hate one and love the other or be loyal to one and despise the other. You cannot serve both. I believe that money does have spiritual dynamics. We know that it has the ability to affect us in either a positive or a negative way. But as long as we are aligning ourselves with God and His principles, we will be entrusted with true riches.

Let's look for a moment at 1 Timothy 6:6-11. Timothy is the Apostle Paul's spiritual son, his disciple, and Paul is giving him some personal instructions as a young man. Paul says that in order to become a mature man of God, Timothy is going to have to learn and understand how to handle money.

> Now godliness with contentment is great gain. For we brought nothing into this world, and it is certain we can carry nothing out. And having food and clothing, with these we shall be content. But those who desire to be rich fall into temptation and a snare, and into many foolish and harmful lusts which drown men in destruction and perdition. For the love of money is a root of all kinds of evil, for which some have strayed from the faith in their greediness, and pierced themselves through with many sorrows.

Paul says godliness with contentment is great gain—*contentment.* We brought nothing into this world and it's certain that we can carry nothing out. Consider that for a moment. Obviously, you've never seen a hearse pulling a U-Haul behind it! It's not about how much you have—the balance in your bank account, your possessions, acquiring more land or things. To be content is to be secure in Christ, to be rightly related to Him, and to know and be assured that God is your provider. He is a good Father and He takes care of His children.

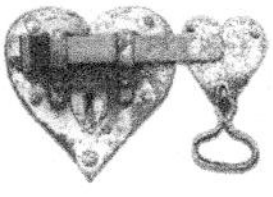

"To be content is to be secure in Christ."

The Apostle Paul talks about contentment in Philippians 4:11-12. "Not that I speak in regard to need, for I have learned in whatever state I am, to be content: I know how to be abased, and I know how to abound. Everywhere and in all things I have learned both to be full and to be hungry, both to abound and to suffer need." Paul was not worried. His focus was not on what he had or didn't have. He had learned to be content in every life situation. How? His focus was on the Lord whom he loved and served, and the things of life had no bearing on his state of mind. He learned contentment in his relationship and trust in the One who gave everything for him.

There is a warning in 1 Timothy 6:9 that says, "But those who desire to be rich fall into temptation and a snare, and into many foolish and harmful lusts which drown men in destruction and perdition."

That was my desire; I wanted to be rich. After graduating from college, being wealthy was my primary focus. And it was definitely a snare. I can certainly say, "Been there, done that!" I'm just thankful that God intercepted me on that path, in my foolishness, and redirected my life.

Verse 10 in the old King James version of the Bible reads, "For the love of money is the root of all evil." It actually leaves out the words "kinds of." The love of money is a root; it's unrighteous mammon which is able to get its claws into you, get your attention and your focus, and capture your heart. There is a spirit attached to money. When your heart goes after money, you stray from truth and godliness: "while some coveted after, they have erred from the faith and pierced themselves through with many sorrows" (1 Timothy 6:10).

God's answer is found in verses 11 and 12. "But you, O man of God, flee these things and pursue righteousness, godliness, faith, love, patience, gentleness. Fight the good fight of faith, lay hold on eternal life, to which you were also called and have confessed the good confession in the presence of many witnesses." Do you know what flee means? It means RUN. Run and pursue righteousness, godliness, faith, love, patience, and gentleness. Align your life with the Word of God. Make known your confession before others. Pursue Christ. Hold on to eternal things to which you have been called.

Be a faithful steward of the things of God. You cannot serve God and mammon. It just won't work. Understand the danger of chasing after riches. Money is not evil; it's the love of money that is. There is an interesting command and an inherent promise in the last few verses of this chapter:

> Command those who are rich in this present age not to be haughty, nor to trust in uncertain riches but in the living God, who gives us richly all things to enjoy. Let them do good, that they be rich in good works, ready to give, willing to share, storing up for themselves a good foundation for the time to come, that they may lay hold on eternal life. –1 Timothy 6:17-19

This is our charge and His command—not to put our trust in uncertain riches, but in the living God who gives us richly all things to enjoy.

True Riches

What does it mean to be rich? How do you qualify or quantify what it takes to be considered wealthy? You know of people, maybe personally, who are millionaires or even billionaires. When you compare the balance in your checkbook with theirs, you'd probably say you are not rich. However, if you look at the rest of the world and how people live in places like India, China, and parts of Africa or Central and South America, and compare their standard of living to ours—then we're definitely rich!

I've traveled all over the world and been to many of those places, and I can tell you—they have practically nothing. It's extremely difficult;

millions of people live in poverty. In comparison, we ARE rich, not just in material wealth, but in so many other ways.

Consider prayer, the Good News of the Gospel, the power of the Holy Spirit—the list could go on. God is a rewarder of those who faithfully steward what has been given to them. The command says, "those who are rich in this present age [are] not to be haughty" or high-minded. What that means is to think soberly about your financial situation and all that you possess. Don't put your trust in uncertain riches. And don't think that you have gotten to this place of wealth, or a place of poverty, solely on your own efforts. Uncertain riches are uncertain; you can't trust your bank account or certainly not the stock market.

We live in a world that abounds in sin, and mammon has a spirit attached to it. It's constantly trying to grab your heart and pull you into its web. Proverbs 23:4-5 says,

> Do not overwork to be rich;
>
> Because of your own understanding, cease!
>
> Will you set your eyes on that which is not?
>
> For riches certainly make themselves wings;
>
> They fly away like an eagle toward heaven.

Let me tell you, I've seen thousands of dollars just fly away! I've proven those Scriptures in the Bible, maybe not all 2,300, but a whole bunch—the bad ones and the good ones.

You can, however, trust in the living God. There's no permanent stability or guarantee in anything else other than Jesus and His Word. He is the Rock. Things will be shaken; in fact, the Bible says that everything that can be shaken will be shaken.

Look at 1 Timothy 6:17 again. It says God gives us richly all things to enjoy! Isn't that amazing? Sometimes we think that God doesn't want us to have things. No. He is saying He wants to give us good things to enjoy. That's His heart; He is a good Father and provider. Are we any different? I'm a father and I love my kids. I want them to be blessed, enjoy their life, and have an abundance. The only issue is that God wants us not to be bound by money or possessions but to realize that every good and perfect gift truly comes from Him. He wants our affection and for us to be totally devoted to Him and to have a heart like His.

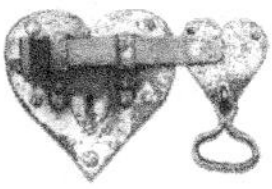

"The heart of God the Father is to give—lavishly."

John 16:33 says, "These things I have spoken to you, that in Me you may have peace. In the world you will have tribulation; but be of good cheer, I have overcome the world." So don't fear! This world has no stability in it. We are faced with sin, sickness, death, and tribulation, but Jesus Christ is our Rock and our Anchor and our Peace. In Him is perfect peace.

It's time for us as a church and a people to "be rich in good works, ready to give, willing to share." We need to become givers. He freely gave it all, the greatest gift that He could give—His Son. Out of His love for each of us, He gave, so that we could have the fullness of the inheritance in Christ Jesus. Now we can freely give.

Determine in your heart to be a lavish giver, to bless others, and to faithfully steward all that He has given you and put your trust in His unfailing love for you.

TAKE IT TO HEART

Becoming a steward of God's resources and all that means may be a new concept to you. As you have read through this chapter on getting God's perspective, you may have been challenged to delve deeper into your beliefs about money and managing finances, the spirit of mammon, and what it means to be a generous, lavish giver. Take a moment to sit with the Father and ask Him to give you His heart and understanding about these principles and how He wants to demonstrate His love, provision, and promises through your life.

TAKE IT TO GOD

I take this moment, Father, to acknowledge that "The earth is the Lord's and the fullness thereof." It's all Yours. You're the owner of it all; in charge of all things.

I pray and ask You to forgive me, Lord, for thinking that the money and resources that I have are mine alone and not considering that You've placed them in my possession to steward and manage according to Your Word. Please forgive me for not being faithful in the little. I want to walk in Your will and Your way. I want to see Your Kingdom come on earth as it is in Heaven. May I be a vessel of blessing to the world around me and a reflection of Your love. I give You permission, Holy Spirit, to lead me in the everlasting way. In Jesus's name. Amen.

CHAPTER ONE

SCRIPTURE REFERENCES

Haggai 2:8

Psalm 50:10

John 1:1-2

Luke 16:10-13

Luke 21:1-4

1 Timothy 6:6-11

Philippians 4:11-12

1 Timothy 6:17-19

Proverbs 23:4-5

John 16:33

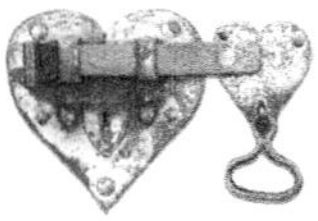

God is After our Heart

The greatest treasures we can ever find are those which have infinite and indisputable value. The Bible speaks of many, highlighting their importance in the life of a Christ-follower. These are faith, hope, love, integrity, wisdom, truth, and character, among others. We find in Matthew 6:19-21 the battle between good and evil, Heaven and the world: "Do not lay up for yourselves treasures on earth, where moth and rust destroy and where thieves break in and steal; but lay up for yourselves treasures in heaven, where neither moth nor rust destroys and where thieves do not break in and steal. For where your treasure is, there your heart will be also." The heart of every believer is tried and weighed in the things that we cherish, focus on, give our resources to, and treasure.

> *"The heart of every believer is tried and weighed in the things that we cherish."*

God makes it clear that the things which we can touch and feel are temporal; they are going to rust and decay, and the enemy can break in, steal, and destroy those treasures. It's not that they are necessarily bad or destructive, but they don't bring eternal value—they're earthly. God is saying to put our focus on heavenly treasures, on things above.

Now, I'm not exactly sure why I need to store up treasures in Heaven. For what purpose? My concept of Heaven tells me that I'm not going to need anything when I get there. I believe there are some dynamics in being faithful with that which is another man's, and God is revealing how we are to steward, give, and to send things on ahead. It's revealing our hearts, and the handling of money and treasures is important now and will be where we're headed.

So how do we store up treasures in Heaven? Well, I don't really know, except that at the core is giving. I'm not just talking about money, although that's a part of it, but it's our time, resources, compassion, energy, love, and worship. God gives us all things to enjoy, and He asks that we give from the abundance of our treasury, being rich in good works, by giving ourselves away and by serving others.

It's obvious that the Lord is concerned about the condition of our heart and with our attitudes. There is nothing wrong in having money. God is not after our bank account or our money. I had a pastor friend of mine years ago say, "When God wants your attention, a lot of times He just pulls on your wallet!" That does tend to get our attention because our hearts are connected to our possessions. It's interesting that He doesn't say, "Where your heart is, there will be your treasure." No. It's where your treasure is, that you'll find your heart connected to it. God is after the heart.

Mammon or God

Matthew 6:22-23 reads, "The lamp of the body is the eye. If therefore your eye is good, your whole body will be full of light. But if your eye is bad, your whole body will be full of darkness. If therefore the light that is in you is darkness, how great is that darkness!" When we read this in context and look at the Scripture, we see that it is talking about treasures. Jesus is talking about our focus—what it is upon which we are focused.

We are changed from glory to glory as we behold Him. We are changed by that upon which we focus. The lamp of the body is the eye, and if your eyes focus on light, the Scriptures say that your whole body is going to be light and clear. Conversely, if you're focused on things that are negative, then it's going to produce negative results. This principle applies to everything. It's about focus, because whatever you focus on becomes your place of worship and your heart follows. Yes, wherever your treasure is, there will your heart be also. Our focus should be on God, who is a good Father and generously gives us all things to enjoy.

The struggle is that we can't serve two masters. Many do not believe that, but it's true. "No one can serve two masters; for either he will hate the one and love the other, or else he will be loyal to the one and despise the other. You cannot serve God and mammon" (Matthew 6:24). Our hearts cannot be completely devoted to God if our hearts are focused on money, success, passions, selfish desires, possessions, or anything else. Which master would you prefer to serve?

I don't see anywhere else in Scripture where sin is personified. Here it has a name. Mammon was a Babylonian deity. The word basically means money. So what Jesus is saying here is that there is a competition between God, who is Spirit, and mammon, which has a spirit connection behind it. You have to make a choice. You have to understand that you can't serve both. The spirit of mammon is the enemy who is a liar and a slanderer and wants to rule over you and master you. The devil will do anything he can to get you caught in deception and destroy your life.

Your Worth and Value

Let's look at Matthew 6:25-29. Here is an astounding admonition and encouragement.

> Therefore I say to you, do not worry about your life, what you will eat or what you will drink; nor about your body, what you will put on. Is not life more than food and the body more than clothing? Look at the birds of the air, for they neither sow nor reap nor gather into barns; yet your heavenly Father feeds them. Are you not of more value than they? Which of you by worrying can add one cubit to his stature?
>
> So why do you worry about clothing? Consider the lilies of the field, how they grow: they neither toil nor spin; and yet I say to you that even Solomon in all his glory was not arrayed like one of these.

"Are you not more valuable than the birds of the air?"

"Are you not of more value than they?" This is an interesting question. Do you realize how much we are bombarded with this question of how valuable we are, everyday?

We kill innocent babies by the thousands, but boy if you kill a screech owl or some other endangered species, you're in big trouble. How dare we mistreat an animal, but we are ruthlessly aborting babies and calling it our "right." Do you understand how twisted this whole thing is? It's the same spirit behind mammon.

Are you not more valuable than the birds? YES! Just in case you didn't hear the answer—YES! Another question being asked here is whether being anxious can add one cubit to your stature. Seriously, does worrying do anything positive? Not a bit. It's a thief that comes to steal life from us. It binds us to fear that we will not have enough or that we won't be able to pay our bills, put food on the table, take care of our family, and on and on it goes.

Have you watched the advertisements on TV for retirement plans? Do you have enough? What will you do? Who will take care of you? They will—just invest with them.

That is not what God's Word says. *Consider the lilies of the field.* It's such a powerful declaration here, a promise that the God of the universe cares more for us than anything else and He will provide for all of our needs. He provides for the birds and they don't do a thing. He cares for the flowers and trees that are arrayed with beauty. He creates and causes things to grow for us to enjoy. Then He says, "Don't worry about what you're going to eat or what to wear—I've got this! I love you more than these." And He does. He is a good Father.

In verses 30-32, Jesus underscores His commitment to His children and His desire that we trust Him and be free from worry.

> Now if God so clothes the grass of the field, which today is, and tomorrow is thrown into the oven, will He not much more clothe you, O you of little faith? Therefore do not worry, saying, "What shall we eat?" or "What shall we drink?" or "What shall we wear?" For after all these things the Gentiles seek. For your heavenly Father knows that you need all these things.

His knowing our needs is accompanied by His desire to meet our needs, and in that we can have peace and assurance.

Posture of Prayer

Let's look at Matthew 6:6-8 where Jesus talks about prayer and how to position yourself and your heart.

> But you, when you pray, go into your room, and when you have shut your door, pray to your Father who is in the secret place; and your Father who sees in secret will reward you openly. And when you pray, do not use vain repetitions as the heathen do. For they think that they will be heard for their many words.
>
> Therefore do not be like them. For your Father knows the things you have need of before you ask Him.

When Jesus talks about prayer here, what does He tell them? He says, do not use a bunch of words and ramble on. Realize that your Father in Heaven already knows what you need and everything that is happening. He knows every problem, every concern, the despair, the fear, the broken heart—everything. You don't need to labor over these problems or spend a lot of time praying about them. He knows all the yesterdays, the todays, and the tomorrows. He knows it all, the beginning to the end. He created each of us and He knows our needs. He is a good Father. But He is asking that we trust Him and be content with what we have, what He has given us. He wants our hearts.

Covenant Relationships

In the last verses of Matthew 6, God speaks about a covenant relationship which He has with us. "But seek first the Kingdom of God and His righteousness and all these shall be added to you." When a man and a woman enter into a covenant, it is two people coming together and exchanging their vows. In those vows, each makes promises to the other. In effect, they are committing everything that they have to each other, promising to be there in the good times and the bad, for better or worse, richer or poorer, in sickness and in health.

Marriage is more than an agreement or a contract, although many contracts are binding. It is a spiritual covenant—one in which we enter by faith, with a full-hearted commitment. This covenant in Matthew 6:33 is one between the Father, Jesus, the Holy Spirit, and US! And it's a better covenant, the Word says, based on better promises. It's not based upon our keeping the law or being perfect. No, it's based upon Jesus's finished work on the Cross, having fulfilled all the requirements of the law.

In contrast, Jesus speaks about the Gentiles who are not in covenant. "Therefore, do not worry, saying, 'What shall we eat?' or 'What shall we drink?' For after all these things the Gentiles seek" (Matthew 6:31-32). The Gentiles were not Jews, and He is saying that they have reason to worry and had better hustle because they do not have a covenant-with God promising to take care of them.

In the story of the woman from Canaan, Jesus is amazed by the faith of this woman, a Gentile who is not in covenant. The disciples are disturbed because she is bothering Jesus, and they want Him to send her away.

> And His disciples came and urged Him, saying, "Send her away, for she cries out after us." But He answered and said, "I was not sent except to the lost sheep of the house of Israel." Then she came and worshiped Him, saying, "Lord, help me!" But He answered and said, "It is not good to take the children's bread and throw it to the little dogs." And she said, "Yes, Lord, yet even the little dogs eat the crumbs which fall from their masters' table." Then Jesus answered and said to her, "O woman, great is your faith! Let it be to you as you desire." And her daughter was healed from that very hour. –Mathew 15:22-28

> ***"God is a covenant-keeping God who loves without limits."***

The message Jesus wants to convey is clear. The Father will take care of His children. He has not held back one thing. He has given us the greatest gift—His Son. He has withheld nothing. He is a covenant-keeping God, He loves without limits, and we are heirs of His Kingdom. It's all a byproduct of our relationship with Him; it's a part of the package deal.

Seek Him First

It has to begin with putting Him first. We must set our heart and our gaze upon Him, to seek first the Kingdom advancement and a right relationship with Him. If we do, He promises that *all these things shall be added to you.*

What does it mean to seek the Lord? It means to look for, long for, and to wait for His presence. In Hebrew, the translation for presence is *face*, and that means to be before Him, with Him, focused on Him. It's a setting of the mind and heart on God; it's a conscious effort to fix our attention and affection on Him.

God's love for us is infinite and more than anything else, He wants to be in an intimate relationship with us and to capture our hearts. He wants us free from the love of mammon and its destructiveness and the fear of not having enough. He wants us to trust Him for our tomorrows and not be bound up in anxiety and worry about our basic needs. The Psalmist declares, "I have been young, and now am old; / Yet I have not seen the righteous forsaken, / Nor his descendants begging bread" (Psalm 37:25).

Yes, tomorrow will have worries and trouble. We don't know what will happen tomorrow, next week, or next year. We live in a fallen world and the enemy is the thief of our past and our tomorrows, always trying to steal, kill, and destroy.

But Jesus has come to set us free and give us an abundant life. He invites us into a love relationship with Him that He might pour out upon all of His sons and daughters the blessings He has stored up in Heaven. *"If you seek Him, He will be found by you"* (1 Chronicles 28:9).

God wants to set each one of us free—free from mammon and worry and focusing on things of the flesh and earthly things. It begins with repentance and acknowledging that the things of this world have had a grip upon our lives and have bound us to lies about God's love, goodness, and provision.

TAKE IT TO HEART

God is a perfect Father, unlike even the most extraordinary earthly father. His love is from everlasting to everlasting. You have been given an opportunity to step into a deep, personal relationship with the God of the universe. As you consider the nature of this covenant, let me encourage you to take that step and to trust Him fully. He is waiting to pour out His blessings upon you and richly give you *all things to enjoy.* Especially Him.

TAKE IT TO GOD

Dear God, I repent of allowing fear to control my life and my decisions; for focusing on all these earthly things and letting mammon (money) be my master. I ask You to forgive me for not believing that You are good and not trusting in Your sovereign ways in my life and heart. I yield up to You my unbelief, my wrong mindsets, my doubts and fears, and all my misplaced affections.

I ask You, Lord, to renew my heart and spirit and turn my gaze toward You. I want to see You high and lifted up, to see You as You really are—the living, almighty God of Heaven and earth who loves me without measure and has promised a deep abiding relationship as I seek first Your Kingdom.

I love You, I give You praise, and I thank You for all that You have yet planned for me in an extraordinary, blessed life as Your child. In Jesus's name. Amen.

CHAPTER TWO

SCRIPTURE REFERENCES

Matthew 6:19-21

Matthew 6:22-23

Matthew 6:25-29

Matthew 6:6-8

Matthew 6:31-33

Matthew 15:22-28

Matthew 6:24

Matthew 6:30-32

Psalm 37:25

1 Chronicles 28:9

3

Principle of First Things

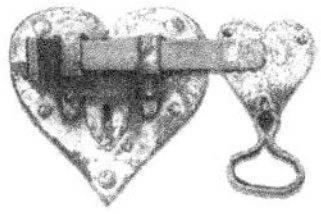

The principle of first things runs throughout the Scriptures. In fact, the Bible references firstfruits, first things, or devoted things no less than thirty-two times. This is foundational to having a successful, blessed life. Why? Because if God is first in your life, everything else comes into order. Matthew 6:33 states, "But seek first the kingdom of God and His righteousness and all of these things will be added to you." When you keep first things first through faith and obedience, you turn God's promises into provision.

So what is the Kingdom of God that we are to seek? That may seem like a simple question, easily explained in religious terms, but it takes on a deeper meaning when we put it in context of relationship. God reveals that it is about His rule and reign on earth, yes, but also in our hearts. It's a different operating system than the world's, concerning how we look at life, how we make decisions, how we manage our resources, how we conduct business, and even how we love.

The Father wants us to understand that it's all His to begin with. He uses strong words in the Hebrew, saying, "It is Mine; My property; it belongs to Me." He is giving us stewardship over the earth and all it possesses. However, He is asking, mandating, that we manage it according to His ways—according to Kingdom principles, not the world's.

How? How do we steward? How do we store up treasures in Heaven? How do we make sure our treasures are not on earth? We begin by seeking Him with all our heart. We make Him our focus every

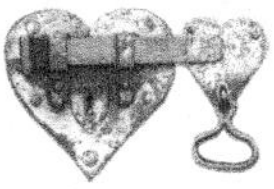

"Where are your treasures stored?"

day, in prayer, in worship, in our time in His Word. Our eyes and our hearts turn toward God, and we wait to hear His Word eternal spoken to us. And out of that relationship, we understand His ways.

In one very important way, we can see the promise that God has laid out in Proverbs 3:9-10: "Honor the Lord with your possessions and with the firstfruits of all your increase, so your barns will be filled with plenty and your vats will overflow with new wine." Honor the Lord with your possessions; with the firstfruits of ALL your increase. It's a powerful promise, isn't it? If we honor Him, make Him first, seek Him, then He will add to our lives everything we need and more.

The Heart Condition

Let's look for a minute at a story of Cain and Abel in Genesis 4:1-5 about this principle.

> Now Adam knew Eve his wife, and she conceived and bore Cain, and said, "I have acquired a man from the LORD." Then she bore again, this time his brother Abel. Now Abel was a keeper of sheep, but Cain was a tiller of the ground. And in the process of time it came to pass that Cain brought an offering of the fruit of the ground to the LORD. Abel also brought of the firstborn of his flock and of their fat. And the LORD respected Abel and his offering, but He did not respect Cain and his offering. And Cain was very angry, and his countenance fell.

Verses 6-8 continue:

> So the LORD said to Cain, "Why are you angry? And why has your countenance fallen? If you do well, will you not be accepted? And if you do not do well, sin lies at the door. And its desire is for you, but you should rule over it."
>
> Now Cain talked with Abel his brother; and it came to pass, when they were in the field, that Cain rose up against Abel his brother and killed him.

We use this story from the Bible in our Free Indeed seminar when we talk about open doors. The enemy is vicious in his attempts to get us angry or upset—an open door—and to act out of those places of sin and brokenness. Here we learn that Cain killed his brother out of jealousy and revenge.

Abel kept sheep and Cain was a farmer. They both understood the purpose of the firstfruits and offerings to the Lord. Abel, following God's command, brought the firstborn of his *flock and of their fat*, which means that he brought the first and the best as an offering. Cain brought an offering of the fruit of the ground. However, it says that *"in the process of time it came to pass,"* which has been implied that Cain brought his offering sometime later and it was possibly not firstfruits. Hebrews 11:4 says that Abel's was the more excellent sacrifice because it was offered in faith. It was the state of their hearts that made the difference, though Cain's may have been a scanty gift of common produce and not of firstfruits.

The question is really where you are in your acknowledgement of God as provider. God is saying that He wants to be first in our lives—first in everything. He asks us to consecrate the firstborn as we see in Exodus 13: "whatever opens the womb among the children of Israel, both of man and beast." This is one way to store up treasures in Heaven. By offering firstfruits to God of our time, our resources, or our increase, we honor Him and put our trust in His goodness and absolute trustworthiness to provide for all of our needs, as long as we steward what He has given.

Let's take a moment to look further at Exodus 13:11-15.

> And it shall be when the LORD brings you into the land of the Canaanites, as He swore to you and your fathers, and gives it to you, that you shall set apart to the LORD all that open the womb, that is, every firstborn that comes from an animal which you have; the males shall be the LORD's. But every firstborn of a donkey you shall redeem with a lamb; and if you will not redeem it, then you shall break its neck. And all the firstborn of man among your sons you shall redeem. So it shall be, when your son asks you in time to come, saying, "What is this?" that you shall say to him, "By strength of hand the LORD brought us out of Egypt, out of the house of bondage. And it came to pass, when Pharaoh was stubborn about letting us go, that the LORD killed all the firstborn in the land of Egypt, both the firstborn of man and the firstborn of beast. Therefore I sacrifice to the LORD all males that open the womb, but all the firstborn of my sons I redeem."

Most of us remember the story of the Passover. The children of Israel were to kill a lamb and put the blood over their doorposts and lintels of their houses. When the death angel came, it would see the blood and pass over that place, and the destroyer was not allowed to enter. This was a horrible event; all the firstborn in Egypt died, whether human or animal, and there was great weeping and wailing. But that is what God had prescribed. It's a serious principle that God wants us to understand. He doesn't want our leftovers. We are to bring the first of everything, and that begins with seeking Him first. If we want to experience God's highest rewards, then we have to follow His principles.

This principle of firstfruits was sovereignly, eternally, set into place by God, the Father, giving His firstborn Son, Jesus, to die on the Cross for each one of us. He demonstrated how we are to give and love by not even sparing His own Son. Jesus was the sacrifice, the spotless Lamb slain for the world. In His death, He paid the price for our wickedness and sin and redeemed us from the sentence of death.

"Jesus was the firstfruits sacrifice of the Father."

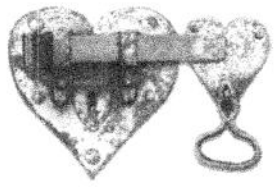

Colossians 1:15-18 says:

> He is the image of the invisible God, the firstborn over all creation. For by Him all things were created that are in heaven and that are on earth, visible and invisible, whether thrones or dominions or principalities or powers. All things were created through Him and for Him. And He is before all things, and in Him all things consist. And He is the head of the body, the church, who is the beginning, the firstborn from the dead, that in all things He may have the preeminence.

God led by example in Jesus. He is the firstborn over all creation. He was the sacrifice and the firstborn from the dead. This is the principle laid out again in Leviticus 27:28-33 which defines redeeming persons and property dedicated to God:

> Nevertheless no devoted offering that a man may devote to the Lord of all that he has, both man and beast, or the field of his possession, shall be sold or redeemed; every devoted offering is most holy to the Lord. No person under the ban, who may become doomed to destruction among men, shall be redeemed, but shall surely be put to death. And all the tithe of the land, whether of the seed of the land or of the fruit of the tree, is the Lord's. It is holy to the Lord. If a man wants at all to redeem any of his tithes, he shall add one-fifth to it.

> And concerning the tithe of the herd or the flock, of whatever passes under the rod, the tenth one shall be holy to the LORD. He shall not inquire whether it is good or bad, nor shall he exchange it; and if he exchanges it at all, then both it and the one exchanged for it shall be holy; it shall not be redeemed.

This may be one of the reasons why we don't read Leviticus very often—it's tough stuff! But here again, in these verses, God is saying that His ways are not our ways and His thoughts are not our thoughts. You would never find God saying, "Oh, I never thought of that!" He has thought out everything from before time and into eternity. He is omniscient, omnipotent, and omnipresent. We just need to come to a place of trusting Him, giving Him honor, and making Him first and pre-eminent in all things. If we do that, and live by the principles in His Word, we will see all that we've given to Him redeemed.

Do you recall the story of Jericho in Joshua 6 when the children of Israel marched around the city blowing trumpets and worshipping? The city of Jericho miraculously fell, but God told them not to take any of the spoils. He said, "Jericho is Mine, and I want you to kill everyone there and bring all the silver and the gold back and put it in the treasury of the Lord. It's Mine." Why? Because it was the first city in the Promised Land to be captured—firstfruits! But things went south. A person in the camp, named Achan, took some devoted possessions for himself.

Then the Israelites went to conquer Ai and they were defeated. Joshua went before the Lord and asked God what was going on because God told them they would have victory. God revealed that there was sin in their camp and that someone had taken the cursed things.

So Joshua called the heads of all the households together and Achan confessed, saying he had coveted the silver and stolen from the Lord the devoted things. As a result of that disobedience and deception, Achan and his whole family were stoned to death. This place was marked with a heap of stones which the Bible says *is still there to this day* and is called the Valley of Achor.

A Mindset of Giving

In the next chapter, we will deal with the question of tithing in depth, but I wanted to give an introduction to this subject and share with you a story that I heard from Bishop Joseph Garlington, the founder of Covenant Church of Pittsburg, Pennsylvania, a multiracial, cross-cultural community of believers.

Bishop Garlington talked about impoverished neighborhoods and the churches in those areas. He said, "I talk about money and I try to get our people into a mindset of giving and tithing. I tell them, look, if you have got God's money in your pocket, watch out, your leg may just blow right off. That 'devoted' thing is going to be burned up; it's going to be destroyed. If you've got God's money in your bank account, it may just burn up, too." He said he would have people coming by the church in the middle of the night to slide their money under the door! Ha-ha—not sure that's the best way to teach about tithing! However, the point is to understand the principle of the tithe. Whether it's the seed of the land or the fruit of the tree, it is the Lord's and holy unto Him, meant to be dedicated to Him.

God considers the tithe as holy, which means it is set apart and sanctified. In Deuteronomy 26:1-2, God says,

> And it shall be, when you come into the land which the LORD your God is giving you as an inheritance, and you possess it and dwell in it, that you shall take some of the first of all the produce of the ground, which you shall bring from your land that the LORD your God is giving you, and put it in a basket

> and go to the place where the LORD your God chooses to make His name abide . . . then you shall say before the LORD your God: "I have removed the holy tithe from my house, and also have given them to the Levite, the stranger, the fatherless, and the widow, according to all Your commandments which You have commanded me; I have not transgressed Your commandments, nor have I forgotten them. I have not eaten any of it when in mourning, nor have I removed any of it for an unclean use, nor given any of it for the dead. I have obeyed the voice of the LORD my God, and have done according to all that You have commanded me."

Even 430 years before the Mosaic Law established tithing, Abraham and Jacob gave tithes to God, out of their heart and with appreciation for the goodness of God in their lives. Tithing is indeed a heart thing. God knows that our heart is attached to treasures, and He wants to be our most treasured possession. It's an act of honoring Him, trusting Him, and acknowledging that all the provisions we have ultimately come from His hand. He wants to sanctify and redeem what we tithe back to Him and bless us abundantly. Yes, He is a good, good Father.

> And concerning the tithe of the herd or the flock, of whatever passes under the rod, the tenth one shall be holy to the LORD. He shall not inquire whether it is good or bad, nor shall he exchange it; and if he exchanges it at all, then both it and the one exchanged for it shall be holy; it shall not be redeemed.
> –Leviticus 27:32-33

This Scripture had clear meaning to the people of Israel, who were largely an agrarian society and economy, which is different from what most of us today are engaged in. The requirement of the tithe was understood. The first sheep which passed by was to be the Lord's and taken out of the fold and killed as an offering. But imagine you're a sheep herder and you're thinking, "Nobody is looking, and that seventh one is kind of lame. I think I'll just pull a switch and offer him. We're going to kill it anyway; why kill a perfectly good lamb?" This reasoning does not align with God's. He says that man's ways are not His ways. True, it may not make sense, especially if you're looking at this as a business. What if most of the sheep are lame, but God gets the good ones? That's a problem.

"God's provision is linked to our obedience."

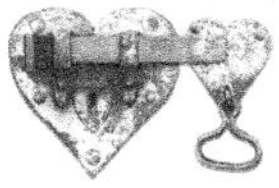

Tithing is directly related to the cycle of blessings and abundance. God does not want to withhold. He has good things in store for His children and He is faithful, but His provision is linked to our stewardship and our commitment to honor and obey His principles in His Word.

Unique Provision

In 1 Kings 17:1-16, we have a story about Elijah, the Tishbite.

> And Elijah the Tishbite, of the inhabitants of Gilead, said to Ahab, "As the LORD God of Israel lives, before whom I stand, there shall not be dew nor rain these years, except at my word."
>
> Then the word of the LORD came to him, saying, "Get away from here and turn eastward, and hide by the Brook Cherith, which flows into the Jordan. And it will be that you shall drink from the brook, and I have commanded the ravens to feed you there."
>
> So he went and did according to the word of the LORD, for he went and stayed by the Brook Cherith, which flows into

> the Jordan. The ravens brought him bread and meat in the morning, and bread and meat in the evening; and he drank from the brook. And it happened after a while that the brook dried up, because there had been no rain in the land.

That's not a good situation! This is one of those stories in the Bible where you come away not really understanding what this is all about. Let me put this into perspective in a personal way.

How often have you been in situations or seasons where you were convinced that God had spoken to you, given direction, and told you something that you were to do? You followed through. And things seemed to be working, and you felt confident that you had heard from Him. Then, unbelievably, the bottom fell out; the creek dried up. Perhaps it was a job, a career path, a new relationship, a donation to a ministry, or a move. What seemed to be the right thing, showing promise, abruptly ended. It was gone. But as we see in the next verses, God was still faithful. Yes, the brook dried up, but God gave Elijah an addition to the word that was spoken (verses 8-12):

> Then the word of the LORD came to him, saying, "Arise, go to Zarephath, which belongs to Sidon, and dwell there. See, I have commanded a widow there to provide for you." So he arose and went to Zarephath. And when he came to the gate of the city, indeed a widow was there gathering sticks. And he called to her and said, "Please bring me a little water in a cup, that I may drink." And as she was going to get it, he called to her and said, "Please bring me a morsel of bread in your hand."
>
> So she said, "As the LORD your God lives, I do not have bread, only a handful of flour in a bin, and a little oil in a jar; and see, I am gathering a couple of sticks that I may go in and prepare it for myself and my son, that we may eat it, and die."

Here again, this does not look like much provision. How many times have we lamented over similar circumstances? The finances have dried up, the job has been cut, the car repairs are outside the budget, and there's no hope and no money. We live in a world and a time when economies are up and economies are down and things feel very uncertain, not secure. Then we lose our job, or COVID hits, and things are closed up and shut down. Life becomes very difficult, and we find ourselves in despair.

My brother is a perfect example of this. He lives in California and was working for a company in Dallas that employed nearly seven thousand workers. Their company made $1 to $2 billion dollars a year in sales in the convention business. It was a phenomenal business, extremely profitable. Then COVID hit and the company crashed and had nothing in sales. Zero! They went from $1.7 billion a year to absolutely nothing. They chose to keep about two hundred people on board, but everyone else was let go. The bottom line is, you can't trust in mammon, man, or the system. You just can't put your hope and trust in temporal things.

I'm sure this widow was in despair. There may have been times when you felt like she did—that there was no way out and no turning this situation into something positive. If you live by looking at your bank account or your 401(k), if you're trusting in your job or your ability to make things happen, you'll probably be extremely disappointed at some point. The enemy comes to steal, kill, and destroy—we've seen that happen again and again. But if our heart and our focus is on earthly things, we will not have the provision or protection over our resources that are held in God's treasury and account for us.

In verse 13 Elijah says to her: "Do not fear; go and do as you have said, but make me a small cake from it first, and bring it to me; and afterward make some for yourself and your son." Why does he say, "Do not fear?" Because fear is the enemy that puts you in bondage and unbelief. Fear says, "I can't give; I don't have enough; there'll be nothing left for me; you don't understand."

Elijah acknowledges her fear but challenges her to respond to his request "first . . . bring it to me." Here, in verses 14-15, is that principle of honoring God, obeying, and trusting that He will provide.

> For thus says the LORD God of Israel: "The bin of flour shall not be used up, nor shall the jar of oil run dry, until the day the LORD sends rain on the earth." So she went away and did according to the word of Elijah; and she and he and her household ate for many days. The bin of flour was not used up, nor did the jar of oil run dry, according to the word of the LORD which He spoke by Elijah.

Fear is the enemy and the spirit of mammon lies to us and wants to keep God's people in servanthood to it. Fear promises fulfillment and success, riches and happiness, but it delivers nothing. God offers us true peace, provision, joy, and a covenantal relationship with Him. His love is everlasting. All the more reason to honor Him with all our possessions and bring before Him our firstfruits.

♥ TAKE IT TO HEART

You may have found yourself in difficult situations where resources were just not there, and you were facing very hard decisions or were in the depths of fear and despair. You are not alone. Throughout the Word of God, He reveals in the stories and the promises that He hears our cries and is faithful to meet our needs. Perhaps it's time to re-think and re-evaluate the beliefs and foundation upon which you have been living your life. Take a few minutes to pray and ask God to reveal any areas where your heart and soul have not been in alignment with His.

TAKE IT TO GOD

Dear God, There are so many areas where I've allowed fear to grip me and the spirit of mammon to control my decisions and hold me captive. Forgive me for making my focus on earthly things and not the Kingdom, for not seeking You first and giving You the place of honor in my life that You deserve.

Thank You for loving me and for Your abundant provision for all my needs, according to Your riches in glory by Christ Jesus. Help me to understand how to be a servant and a faithful steward of all You've given to me. Create in me a true heart of giving that I might give and not withhold out of fear.

I release my heart and put my trust in Your goodness over my life. In Jesus's name. Amen.

CHAPTER THREE

SCRIPTURE REFERENCES

Matthew 6:33

Proverbs 3:9-10

Genesis 4:1-5

Hebrews 11:4

Exodus 13:1-2, 11-15

Colossians 1:15-18

Leviticus 27:28-33

Deuteronomy 26:1-2

1 Kings 17:1-16

100
LB45440078L
100

Tithes and Offerings

We cannot talk about finances without talking about tithing. God's plan from the beginning was to provide for His people using the tithe. Because of the law of sowing and reaping, we can participate in sowing the seeds of finances He gives us, and reap a harvest so that we can be a blessing to others. The word tithe comes from an Old English root meaning one tenth. It is the English translation for the Old Testament Hebrew *asar* word group. The tithe was an offering to the Lord as an expression of thanksgiving and dedication. In the Old Testament agricultural economy, tithes were paid not in cash or gold but in crops or livestock, for only the agricultural fruit of the promised land was to be tithed—not other forms of income. Tithes were given by the patriarchs Abraham and Jacob. A system of tithes was instituted in the Law of God given through Moses, and the prophets rebuked the children of Israel for failing to give the tithe to God.

> For I am the Lord, I do not change; Therefore you are not consumed, O sons of Jacob. Yet from the days of your fathers you have gone away from My ordinances and have not kept them. Return to Me, and I will return to you, says the Lord of hosts. But you said, "In what way shall we return?" Will a man rob God? Yet you have robbed Me! But you say, "In what way have we robbed You?" In tithes and offerings. You are cursed with a curse, for you have robbed Me, even this whole nation. –Malachi 3:6-9

The prophet Malachi wrote those ancient words during a time of great hardship in Israel, when God's people were literally putting themselves into bondage just to survive (Nehemiah 5:1–5). Overwhelmed by painful circumstances, the people allowed a carnal mind to rule. They began to reason, "How can we give offerings and tithes to God when we're under such duress?" So, they stopped giving those tithes.

Throughout the Old Testament, we read historical accounts of kings and their kingdoms, especially the kings of Israel, who came under severe judgement and hardship because they had ceased tithing or honoring the Sabbath and the Lord. The children of Israel were taken captive to Babylon because they were in such disobedience to God and His ways. But every time there was prosperity and revival in Israel, it was because they had restored the tithe and the priesthood and re-established the Sabbath as a holy day unto the Lord.

Let's stop here for a minute and focus on God's statement in verse six that *He does not change*. He is the Lord and is the same yesterday, today, and forever, as it says in Hebrews. That is so important because it brings stability and security into our lives. He doesn't wake up moody or change His mind. He is perfect and constant, and we can trust Him. He is good and His goodness is from *everlasting to everlasting.*

I want to clarify that God is not going around cursing people. Just the opposite. He wants to bless and His desire is to provide a way for us to walk in His blessings. As stated, God has given us all the resources to manage and steward for Him, and if we do, we will receive all the increase and provision He has stored up for us.

"It's strange to consider that we may have 'robbed God'."

However, God has laid out principles to follow. If we stay within His prescribed ordinances and His desire for us, we will remain within His realm of blessing. It's strange to consider that we may have "robbed God," but

He addresses this in saying that His expectation is that everyone—the whole nation—must bring all the tithes into the storehouse that there may be food in His house, and He can therefore bless His people.

> Bring all the tithes into the storehouse, that there may be food in My house, and try Me now in this, says the LORD of hosts, if I will not open for you the windows of heaven and pour out for you such blessing that there will not be room enough to receive it. And I will rebuke the devourer for your sakes, so that he will not destroy the fruit of your ground, nor shall the vine fail to bear fruit for you in the field, says the LORD of hosts; and all nations will call you blessed, for you will be a delightful land, says the LORD of hosts. –Malachi 3:10-12

> Honor the LORD with your possessions, and with the firstfruits of all your increase; so your barns will be filled with plenty, and your vats will overflow with new wine. –Proverbs 3:8-10

> And all the tithe of the land, whether of the seed of the land or of the fruit of the tree, is the LORD's. It is holy to the LORD.
> –Leviticus 27:30

Purpose of the Tithe in the Old Testament

There are three tithes talked about in the Old Testament:

1. The Levitical or sacred tithe (Numbers 18:21, 24)
2. The tithe of the feasts (Deuteronomy 14:22-27)
3. The tithe for the poor (Deuteronomy 14:28, 29)

The first tithe was given to the Levites and priests for their service to God, His people, and the temple, the Tabernacle. They did not own land or have any inheritance, so God ordained that the first

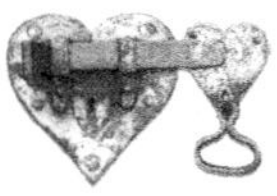

"A second tithe was for a savings plan—a vacation."

tenth should go to them. It is this tithe that we continue to give under today, the priesthood of Melchizedek in the New Testament, consecrated to God for the purpose of furthering the Gospel of the Lord Jesus Christ. This is how you give to your local church so they can equip you to do the work of ministry.

The second tithe was like a savings plan. It was designated or set aside to make sure that the families and households in Israel could travel to Jerusalem for the Passover and the major feasts, like the Tabernacles and Pentecost, and enjoy their time together. It was to be a spiritually refreshing time. This tithe was collected three times a year.

The third tithe was a yearly tithe collected in the third year and designated specifically for the poor. Sometimes this is called a Benevolence Offering today. This was for the fatherless, and the widow.

When looking at all of this tithing you might say, "Wow, that's a lot of giving—that's a lot of money!" True, if you are thinking that the money belongs to you, that it's yours. But it's God's and He has given it to you to steward and to manage, and this is how He wants it spent. The beautiful result is held within the promise He makes that if we honor Him and follow His ways, He will "open the windows of Heaven and pour out a blessing on you that cannot be contained." Do you believe it? Are you willing to take Him at His Word?

God says that when we tithe, it unlocks something in the spiritual realm that enables God to start taking action on our behalf. He works through our yielding and our trusting Him to provide for our lives. He redeems what we give to Him and multiplies it so that 90 percent of what we have goes further than what 100 percent would. You know, I took a lot of math classes in college, and that does not make sense financially, but I know it works. His Word works!

Let's be honest, God doesn't need your money. He owns it all. He owns the cattle on a thousand hills. He uses gold to pave streets in Heaven. God declares: "Every beast of the forest is mine, the cattle on a thousand hills. I know all the birds of the hills, and all that moves in the field is mine. If I were hungry, I would not tell you, for the world and its fullness are mine" (Psalm 50:10-12).

To the natural mind, it doesn't make sense, especially if a person is struggling to live on their earnings and what they have. People tell me all the time, "I can't tithe; I can barely make it on what I've got now. Why would I give away even more?" That's right, and you know something? You never will, because God's ways are not your ways. It's about understanding that when we line ourselves up with God and His principles, we will find our lives blessed.

I remember a man named Wayne Meyers, an evangelist and preacher, who would often speak at Christ for the Nations Institute. He was a famous missionary and traveled all over the world. He told the story of preaching everything he knew to preach as hard as he could while in Mexico in some more rural areas. He said that the Lord spoke to him one day and said, "You've not preached the whole Gospel, the whole counsel." Wayne answered, "I have preached everything I could think of." But the Lord said, "No, you've not taught them to tithe." "But they don't have anything to tithe," Wayne responded. God said, "That's why you have to teach them to tithe. They're never going to have anything unless they understand My principles on handling My money!"

From that day on, Wayne began to share the principle of the tithe with people and help them walk that out. Believers would bring eggs, chickens, and carrots because that's what they had. He began to see a change as they gave sacrificially and experienced God's provision.

Wayne's life was changed as well. He told another story of a time when he was going somewhere to preach and two guys were to pick him up and drive him there. He asked them before they took off,

"Let me ask you a question—do you tithe?" They both said, "No, no." Wayne said, "Well, I'm getting out of this car, because if you rob from God, you'll surely rob from me!" He had countless stories like this. He was a funny guy and an amazing man of God.

Let's look at Genesis 14:18-20 and consider the relevance of the tithe today in light of this Old Testament passage.

> Then Melchizedek king of Salem brought out bread and wine; he was the priest of God Most High. And he blessed him and said,
>
> "Blessed be Abram of God Most High,
> Possessor of heaven and earth;
> And blessed be God Most High,
> Who has delivered your enemies into your hand."
>
> And he gave him a tithe of all.

Genesis 14 is an action-packed story of war between ancient city-states and kings with a surprising conclusion that connects to Abram, whose name would be changed to Abraham. He is seventy-five years old and would gather up 318 servants to war against the armies who have captured Lot, his nephew, and all of his family and possessions. Abram defeats the armies with God's help and retrieves everything that was lost. On the way home, he is met by a mysterious king and priest of God Most High known as Melchizedek.

Melchizedek brings Abram bread and wine and a blessing from God, declaring that it was not by might that the battle was won. It was by the hand of God. Abram immediately responds by giving ten percent of all the plunder to God's priest. The New Testament says that the Gospel was preached to Abraham. I don't know whether

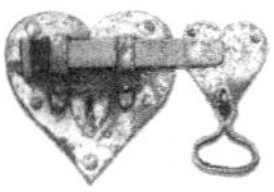

"Long before the Law was given, Abram tithed."

it was at this time or not, but this encounter is later used, in part, to explain the priesthood of Jesus Christ by writers of the New Testament (Hebrews 7:1-8). This speaks of communion. Many commentary writers believe that Melchizedek was probably Jesus incarnate who came to Abram.

Why did Abram offer to Melchizedek a tithe? Where did that thought come from? You know what? It was a response from the heart of a man who understood the things of God. A man who wanted to worship the Lord most High. This was long before the Law was given, and that same heart was transferred down through Isaac and Jacob (Genesis 28:22).

In this passage, Jacob makes a vow to God as he sets up a pillar, calls it Bethel, God's house, and promises to give a tenth of all that the Lord gives him.

God invites us to worship Him and to acknowledge that He is the living God who has good plans for us. He asks that we put our trust in Him and that we place our hope in things above, not in the things of this earth or man.

The Tithe Today

So is the tithe still relevant for today? I hear people say, "Well, you know we're not under the Law any longer; we are in the New Testament now."

Matthew 23:23 says, "Woe to you, scribes and Pharisees, hypocrites! For you pay tithe of mint and anise and cumin, and have neglected the weightier matters of the law: justice and mercy and faith. These you ought to have done, without leaving the others undone." Jesus rebukes the Pharisees because they were trying to do everything just perfectly, and He was saying, "Look, yes, you should have done that, but you've missed the real issue of mercy and all these other things you should be doing." The Pharisees were meticulously focused on making sure they were operating according to the Law. Jesus wasn't saying the tithe was removed; He was pointing out their hypocritical ways.

The transition from the Old Covenant to the New is clear and simple. However, it was accomplished through the agonizing death of Christ on the Cross and His atonement for sin.

From that moment on, there were no more sacrifices for sin because He died once and for all. Animal sacrifices stopped. What about all the rituals and various legal requirements?

Fulfilled in Christ. He was the Lamb of God—the final sacrifice. He fulfilled everything. The Old Testament is fulfilled at the Cross. But what about murder? You're still not supposed to kill. So what happens in the New Testament concerning murder? Does it stop? No, it takes on a higher meaning. Now, the filter becomes "if you have hatred in your heart," you have already committed murder. This applies to adultery and becomes "if you have lust in your heart," you are guilty of adultery. And so with the tithe. When it comes through the Cross, giving becomes an even higher standard.

Let's look at Malachi 3:10. It's very interesting. "Bring all the tithes into the storehouse that there may be food in My house. And try Me now in this," says the LORD of hosts, "If I will not open for you the windows of heaven and pour out for you such blessing that there will not be room enough to receive it."

"Do you realize the tithe is a test?"

I don't believe there is anywhere else in Scripture where God challenges us to test Him. Can you imagine? He is saying, "Test Me in this." So do you realize that the 10 percent tithe is a test? Anytime you find the number ten in the Bible, it's always a test.

There are Ten Commandments. There were ten plagues. There were ten spies who went into the promised land to search it out, and ten virgins. You will find the number ten throughout the Scriptures, and it's always related to a test. Those tests are to prove something. For us, it proves whether or not we are trusting God.

It's a heart test. That's the only thing God is testing—whether you will trust Him, look to Him for provision and to meet your needs, and rely on Him for your tomorrows. As has been said, God already knows your situation, your finances, and your fears, and He longs to satisfy your soul. He wants to be your first love and for you to take Him at His Word. He wants to bless you and fulfill every promise He has made to you as you align your heart with His.

He promises to rebuke the devourer for your sake, so the enemy will not destroy the fruit of the ground or the vine. All the nations will call you blessed because you will be a delightful land. And then He will open the windows of Heaven and pour out a blessing upon you such that there will not be room enough to contain it. I'll bet you've never had a financial advisor give you a promise like that!

You may say that this tithing thing is a hard deal. It can be. It was a challenge for the widow woman who encountered Elijah before preparing her last meal after which she and her son would die (1 Kings 17). It means breaking off the love of money and its entanglements. It means putting God first in finances, not at the end after all the bills have been paid. It's His way, which is higher than ours, and His thoughts as well. He can be trusted. His promise is that when you seek Him first, when you're pursuing Him, then everything else is added into your life. It's part of the covenant relationship with the Lord. It's part of this phenomenal deal!

What is the Storehouse?

There is another question at hand. Where and to whom do you pay the tithe? I use the word pay because it's not really giving. The money belongs to God—it's His. Now, let's look at Deuteronomy 12:5-12 and find out what the Word says.

> But you shall seek the place where the LORD your God chooses, out of all your tribes, to put His name for His dwelling place; and there you shall go. There you shall take your burnt offerings, your sacrifices, your tithes, the heave offerings of your hand, your vowed offerings, your freewill offerings, and the firstborn of your herds and flocks. And there you shall eat before the LORD your God, and you shall rejoice in all to which you have put your hand, you and your households, in which the LORD your God has blessed you.
>
> You shall not at all do as we are doing here today—every man doing whatever is right in his own eyes—for as yet you have not come to the rest and the inheritance which the LORD your God is giving you. But when you cross over the Jordan and dwell in the land which the LORD your God is giving you to inherit, and He gives you rest from all your enemies round about, so that you dwell in safety, then there will be the place where the LORD your God chooses to make His name abide. There you shall bring all that I command you: your burnt offerings, your sacrifices, your tithes, the heave offerings of your hand, and all your choice offerings which you vow to the LORD. And you shall rejoice before the LORD your God, you and your sons and your daughters, your male and female servants, and the Levite who is within your gates, since he has no portion nor inheritance with you.

Malachi 3 says to bring all the tithes into the storehouse. Where is that today? The storehouse is the place where you are fed spiritual food and connected with other believers. Another way of explaining it is as the place where your name is recorded and where you are cared for. This is the place you regularly attend church.

This is an interesting passage. It states clearly that we need to be where God chooses us to be. The issue is not what you like or what suits your fancy. I hear people all the time saying that they are "checking out different churches." They'll visit one for a week or two and then another and point out what they like, or don't like, about each one. I hate to burst your bubble, but the real question is, where does God want you to be? What has He chosen? God has a unique place for every one of us to be connected. It's the place where you are to be fed spiritually, where you're protected, valued, called to serve and to be a part. And—to the point here, it's the place where you are to give your tithe.

"We are living stones being built into a spiritual house."

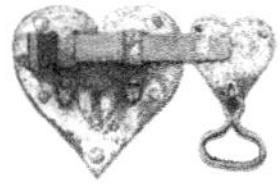

We live in a culture and a time where people float around between churches. The Word does not say we are floating stones. It says we are living stones being built up into a spiritual house—a habitation of the Spirit. We need to be cemented together, deeply committed to one another. I need you and you need me in order to become all that God has for us, His Ecclesia. This is the place which God has prescribed and ordained that you bring your tithe and give support—wherever that local expression of the church gathers. Be faithful and give with a grateful heart, honoring the Lord, and you will be blessed!

TAKE IT TO HEART

The stories of blessings and bountiful provision are endless in the Bible and in the experiences of people who have "tested" God with their finances. He challenges us to see if He won't *open the windows of Heaven and pour out a blessing that you cannot contain*. It's a weighty consideration to begin tithing if that has not been a part of your lifestyle, but God has promised to meet you at that place of a heart commitment. Take some time to pray and ask Him to lead you to a new perspective and freedom in giving.

TAKE IT TO GOD

Dear God, I thank You that You've given Your Word to lead me into truth. It's much clearer now that I have withheld my tithes and offerings and robbed from You. I have not honored You and have neglected to care for Your House. I have trusted in my ways and not Yours. Please forgive me and set me free from my sins and the fears that would hold me captive to this world. You are a good Father, trustworthy, and Your promise is that You will bless and provide beyond anything I can ask or think.

Holy Spirit, I ask you to fill me today with a desire and a joy to bring honor to You with the firstfruits of my increase. My heart is to spend and be spent for souls and the advancement of Your Kingdom (1 Corinthians 12:15). Help me remain faithful. In Jesus's name. Amen.

CHAPTER FOUR

SCRIPTURE REFERENCES

Malachi 3:6-12

Proverbs 3:8-10

Leviticus 27:30

Psalm 50:10-12

Genesis 14:18-20

Hebrews 7:1-8

Genesis 28:22

Matthew 23:23

Deuteronomy 12:5-12

Nehemiah 5:1-5

Numbers 18:21,24

Deuteronomy 14:22-29

1 Kings 17

1 Corinthians 12:15

GIVE
BACK

GIVE
BACK

The Grace of Giving

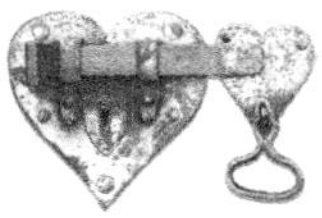

The New Testament, the New Covenant, carries such a contrast to the Old Testament and its laws and legalism. But the New Testament's major theme is GRACE. Although the law is still present to reveal how God wants His church to live and to make us aware of sin, grace does what the law could not do. Grace opens the door for salvation and for us to be declared righteous through the finished work of Christ on the Cross.

This becomes significant as Jesus takes us into a whole new realm of handling finances—a realm of the Spirit where He lays out principles and precepts to govern our handling of resources, time, possessions, relationships, and more.

The Sermon on the Mount in Matthew 5-6 reveals the true heart of God and holds up a high standard for us as well that's meant to be reflected in our love for Christ and His people. But in this message, Jesus rebukes the Pharisees and Sadducees for acting pious and hypocritical. He shows that God is after our hearts, not our adherence to rules. It's not about doing; it's about being.

As we begin this chapter on the grace of giving, I want to take us to 2 Corinthians 8-9, which are all about giving.

> Moreover, brethren, we make known to you the grace of God bestowed on the churches of Macedonia: that in a great trial of affliction the abundance of their joy and their deep poverty abounded in the riches of their liberality. For I bear

> witness that according to their ability, yes, and beyond their ability, they were freely willing, imploring us with much urgency that we would receive the gift and the fellowship of the ministering to the saints. –2 Corinthians 8:1-4

The Apostle Paul wrote 2 Corinthians to celebrate his joy and renewed confidence in his converts. There had been issues, persecutions, a drought, economic strains, and false teachers causing divisions. The letter was also written to inform the Corinthians of Paul's distress as he anxiously awaited news of Titus's mission and to explain why he had failed to make his promised third visit to Corinth. He had wanted to take up an offering for the saints in Jerusalem, so he was appealing to Corinth to provide assistance.

Think about the geography and picture Corinth on a map. It was one of the premier cities of that time, probably like Dallas. Corinth was in Greece. It was a thriving center of business. Macedonia was north of Greece and not very strong or prosperous. There was persecution and a lot of challenges. It had been tough on the believers there, and Paul was expressing how the grace of God on the church in Macedonia had led them to give beyond their ability. They were willing to freely give in ministering to the saints. His encouragement was that their joy abounded through their deep poverty as they gave richly, liberally, out of their lack. In essence, Paul was saying to the church at Corinth, "Listen, guys, get with the program; look at how blessed the Macedonians are because of their heart to give. You said you were going to give; let's do it." And Paul emphasizes that what God is really after is our heart. I love that. It's the principle of firsts here again. First give yourself to the Lord, worship Him, and then give to others by His will.

Verses 6 and 7 say: "So we urged Titus, that as he had begun, so he would also complete this grace in you as well. But as you abound in everything—in faith, in speech, in knowledge, in all diligence, and in your love for us—see that you abound in this grace also."

Do you realize that there is a grace of giving? This is where God wants us to position our hearts. The grace of giving is not just favor. Grace is really the power of God toward we who believe to fulfill His will. Paul says in these seven verses that the church in Corinth had all the gifts (although they did have problems with being out of order), but they abounded in everything—faith, speech, knowledge, diligence, and even in love. But the admonition was for them to make it their focus to abound in grace also.

"God wants us to position our hearts in a grace of giving."

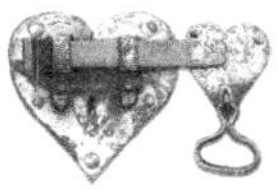

As a believer growing up in church, I never heard about the grace of giving. I didn't understand that it was a gift that God wanted to bestow, empowering us to give. It's the right hand not knowing what the left hand is doing; it's a predisposition to give, a heart that's prepared and eager to give.

Giving is not the same as the tithe. Remember the tithe is the first tenth, the first portion of the increase that belongs to the Lord. Giving is above and beyond the tithe. It's not something that you have to spend hours and hours praying about. You step into a grace of giving, recognizing that God wants to release you and empower you to give and bless others. Acts 20:35 says, "And remember the words of the Lord Jesus, that He said, 'It is more blessed to give than to receive.'" It truly is, and God wants us to learn how to be generous givers.

I was thinking about giving and how to develop a heart to give. I thought, is it any different from learning how to prophesy? Does anyone instantaneously begin to accurately deliver a perfect word? No. In the training and discipleship we offer at church, we tell people that the way to increase a grace gift or its accuracy is to practice and exercise that gift. And connect with people that you can trust and who are seasoned in that gift, who can guide you along the way.

The Sincerity of Love

It's the same thing with giving. We need to develop a sensitivity and awareness of the Lord's leading as we mature in our walk and cultivate a heart for giving according to His will. Start aligning your finances with God's design, begin to honor Him with the tithe, get out of debt, and then you'll be prepared to give. It takes time, but as you grow, so will your desire to give lavishly and to be totally free as a conduit of His resources. We recommend Ramsey Solutions for courses, books and materials to help you get a handle on finances.

It took me a long time to get out of debt—eight years. We ended up with next to nothing, except our home. I had to stop the direction I was going, turn around, and start moving God's way. It took time for my mind to become set on His ways, not the world's, and to put things in order. We finally got there, and so will you. God is faithful.

Take courage and confidence in Jesus Christ who is the same yesterday, today, and forever. He never changes. He is there for you in the long-term, unlimited by time or space.

2 Corinthians 8:8-11 says,

> I speak not by commandment, but I am testing the sincerity of your love by the diligence of others. For you know the grace of our Lord Jesus Christ, that though He was rich, yet for your sakes He became poor, that you through His poverty might become rich. And in this I give advice: It is to your advantage not only to be doing what you began and were desiring to do a year ago; but now you also must complete the doing of it; that as there was a readiness to desire it, so there also may be a completion out of what you have.

This is an amazing verse. Jesus had everything—He was rich—yet He laid down His divinity so that He could take on humanity for us.

I've read a lot of commentaries on this passage, and many of them say it's not really talking about money. If you are any kind of Bible student at all, you know not to take things out of context. Right here in the middle of this whole text, it is talking about money!

When Jesus went to the Cross, He didn't just die so that we could get a ticket to Heaven. Yes, our sins were forgiven, and we gained eternity in that exchange. He died in our place and took on the punishment that was due us, and for that we are forever grateful.

"We gained eternity in the exchange at the Cross."

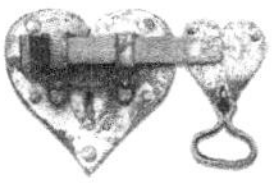

But it also says here that He was rich and for our sakes He became poor, that through His poverty, we might become rich. Isn't that remarkable? These two verses are profound, and we need to stick them on our refrigerator!

This means that He cares for you, and He understands the situation in which you are living. He is a God who gives and operates in great indwelling, abiding grace. He, God Himself, gave His only Son because He so loved the world. It's this same heart and spirit that He longs to imprint upon your heart—that you, too, would become a giver like Him.

Let's pick up verses 12-15.

> For if there is first a willing mind, it is accepted according to what one has, and not according to what he does not have. For I do not mean that others should be eased and you burdened; but by an equality, that now at this time your abundance may supply their lack, that their abundance also may supply your lack—that there may be equality. As it is written, "He who gathered much had nothing left over, and he who gathered little had no lack."

In the New Testament, repentance means to change the way you think. This Scripture is pointing out the obvious: everything that happens starts with a willing mind. This means you have to change your mind. That is what this verse is saying. If you're going to have the grace of giving upon your life, you're going to have to change your mindset—the way you think about money, giving, and stewardship. Paul is saying that you obviously can't give beyond what you have, and you're not expected to give the same amount as someone else. He doesn't want the believers to carry burdens that others could easily carry, but your abundance could supply another's lack. Just to be clear—this is not socialism. That philosophy says that we need to take from everybody who has in order to give to people who don't have, so that we can all have the same amount and be equal. This is Marxism and not what Paul is talking about here.

Karl Marx, a German philosopher, journalist, and socialist revolutionary, saw a problem at the time he was living in France in the mid-nineteenth century. There were very rich, noble people, capitalists, who owned all the property and controlled everything, and everyone else had to work for them. From his view, there was no way to break this cycle, so his solution was to create a way to spread all the resources out evenly so that everyone had the same amount. It's a philosophy that we are seeing being played out today, especially in our educational system and in government. But it's NOT Biblical; it's socialism, communism, and it doesn't work.

In 1990, a group of us got to go to Romania where Communism ruled, just a year after the Iron Curtain came down. It was unbelievable what we saw—shocking. The country seemed frozen in the 1930s in their infrastructure, clothing, everything. And this was better than in Russia, Ukraine, and Georgia. The Communist system did not work.

Giving Freely with Joy

Consider what a stark contrast that is with 1 Timothy that says God gives you richly ALL things to enjoy and that we are to be rich in good works, ready to give and willing to share. And that the heart of every believer in regards to giving should be cheerful.

> Therefore I thought it necessary to exhort the brethren to go to you ahead of time, and prepare your generous gift beforehand, which you had previously promised, that it may be ready as a matter of generosity and not as a grudging obligation.
>
> But this I say: He who sows sparingly will also reap sparingly, and he who sows bountifully will also reap bountifully. So let each one give as he purposes in his heart, not grudgingly or of necessity; for God loves a cheerful giver. And God is able to make all grace abound toward you, that you, always having all sufficiency in all things, may have an abundance for every good work. –2 Corinthians 9:5-8

Allow me to exhort you. Don't let anybody, a pastor or someone in leadership, manipulate you into giving. When you begin to feel that pressure or coercion about giving, then you know they have an agenda. God doesn't manipulate people or twist their arm. Yes, there are times when you feel the burden of the need of the people and your heart will be moved. In those moments, pray and lean in to ask God what He wants you to do. He desires it to be a freewill offering, not an obligation. There are genuine, legitimate needs in the world and the Word says that the poor will always be with us. Let Him direct you. Then give from your heart, when you're ready to give and excited about giving with joy and an awareness of God's leading.

The Lord "loves a cheerful giver. And God is able to make all grace abound toward you, that you, always having all sufficiency in all things, may have an abundance for every good work." The definition of Biblical prosperity is that God is able to cause you to live in such a way that you would abound in everything that you have, and that you would always have enough leftover to be a blessing to someone else's life. Isn't that amazing?!

His kind intention is to meet all your needs—whatever those are—and to supply you with all sufficiency for every good work. He became poor so that we could become rich. That's His gift and His promise to us. As we give Him the first portion, the tithe, and set that apart holy unto Him, He gets involved in the rest, causes it to increase, and bestows upon us the grace of giving. We then give and it is given back to us, "good measure, pressed down, shaken together, and running over" (Luke 6:38).

Continuing, Paul in 2 Corinthians 9:9-11 says, "He has dispersed abroad, He has given to the poor; His righteousness endures forever. Now may He who supplies seed to the sower, and bread for food, supply and multiply the seed you have sown and increase the fruits of your righteousness, while you are enriched in everything for all liberality, which causes thanksgiving through us to God."

This prayer declares that God supplies the seed to the sower and bread for food, and asks that He would now multiply the seed you've sown and increase the fruits of your righteousness. Do you understand what is being said? How do you make bread? You have to first gather and then grind up the wheat or barley (seed). God is going to give you the seed to sow. What's critical here is that you first sow the seed and not eat it. The problem is that most of us have done the opposite—we've eaten our seed and then there is nothing left to sow. Then we find ourselves questioning why things aren't working. It's because we haven't

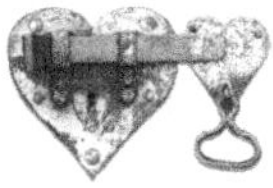

"Sow the seeds God has given to you—don't eat them."

sown or planted the seeds. I've done that as well, saying to myself, "I don't have enough money to pay my bills." Why? Because I've eaten all the seed. This is where we must step into the grace of giving that God wants to infuse into our lives so that we can see things differently and operate by His principles.

> For the administration of this service not only supplies the needs of the saints, but also is abounding through many thanksgivings to God, while, through the proof of this ministry, they glorify God for the obedience of your confession to the gospel of Christ, and for your liberal sharing with them and all men, and by their prayer for you, who long for you because of the exceeding grace of God in you. Thanks be to God for His indescribable gift! –2 Corinthians 9:12-14

Thanks be to God for His indescribable gift! This is remarkable. What happens is that our giving actually causes thanksgiving and increase. Everybody rejoices in giving—it's more blessed to give than to receive. Amen!

Another personal story about increase and provision goes back to when our kids were around thirteen or fifteen, that age range when cars and college were going to become a financial concern. But we had no money for either. We talked about it and I wasn't fretting or stressed out, but I was thinking about what to do and was praying. Did I need to get another job or do something different? I didn't know how we were going to meet the needs, and this had been on my mind for a couple of years. Then one day, God spoke to me. He said, "You're thinking wrong." Hmmm . . . He had said that to me before. That's a pretty normal conversation for us! He said, "You're thinking about how to get." "Yes, Lord," I replied, "I sure am." "You need to think about how to give," He said.

So I went and told Susan that I had this conversation with the Lord and that we needed to start giving more. She said, "Well, where?

How? We've got a budget we're working from. How is that going to happen?" I said, "I don't know, but God spoke to me and it's His ways that work and we need to start giving more." From that day forward, we made a dedicated effort to start giving more. It was amazing how God provided. The kids got vehicles and made it all the way through college without any debt. I look back and I can see so many ways in which God met our needs. He is faithful, faithful, faithful. "The generous soul will be made rich and He who waters will also be watered himself" (Proverbs 11:25).

Proverbs 22:9 is another compelling verse. "He who has a generous eye will be blessed, / For he gives of his bread to the poor." There are many Scriptures throughout the Bible about giving to the poor that we need to take seriously as we embrace His grace of giving. Let's pray.

TAKE IT TO HEART

Grace is a wonderful thing. It feeds our soul and spirit. There are 124 uses of *grace* in the New Testament, eighty-six of which are from the Apostle Paul, who certainly understood the grace of God. John Piper, author, pastor, and theologian, explains grace as "not only a disposition or a quality or an inclination in the nature of God, but an influence or a force or a power or an acting of God that works in us to change our capacities for work and suffering and obedience." Would it not be amazing to live in that place of His grace, especially when it comes to giving and stewarding the resources entrusted to us? Why not pray for that?

TAKE IT TO GOD

Dear God, I earnestly want this grace of giving to be a part of my life and walk with You. I want to have Your heart for the poor, the needy, the building of Your Kingdom, and my life as well. Please forgive me for holding onto my own hurts and fears about provision and the future. Forgive me for withholding blessings and not trusting in Your love. You gave everything for me, and You became poor so that I could share in Your abundance. I ask now for Your empowering presence to help me to become a cheerful, joyful, willing conduit of the riches of Heaven. In Jesus's name. Amen.

CHAPTER FIVE

SCRIPTURE REFERENCES

2 Corinthians 8:1-4

2 Corinthians 8:8-11

Acts 20:35

2 Corinthians 8:12-15

Luke 6:38

2 Corinthians 9:5-8

2 Corinthians 9:12-14

Proverbs 11:25

Proverbs 22:9

Sowing and Reaping

But this I say: He who sows sparingly will also reap sparingly, and he who sows bountifully will also reap bountifully. So let each one give as he purposes in his heart, not grudgingly or of necessity; for God loves a cheerful giver. And God is able to make all grace abound toward you, that you, always having all sufficiency in all things, may have an abundance for every good work.

2 Corinthians 9:6-8

Whether or not you are familiar with agricultural terms or an agrarian lifestyle, the truth is that each one of us is a sower and a reaper. There are principles which govern the earth that God has put into place and which have very discernable outcomes. Sowing and reaping is one of those. Galatians 6:7 says, "Do not be deceived, God is not mocked; for whatever a man sows, that he will also reap."

In the previous chapter, we spent time looking at this verse from 2 Corinthians 9 in light of understanding the grace of giving. Here we are going to delve into the principle of sowing, reaping, and multiplication.

"You always reap what you sow; you reap later than you sow; and, you reap more than you sow!"

In essence, the principle simply stated is this: You always reap what you sow, you reap later than you sow, and you reap more than you sow.

To illustrate the point. If you plant a seed of corn, in about seventy-five days, you will have a stalk of corn with one or two ears of corn, each containing 600 to 900 kernels of corn on each ear. Let's say you have two ears of corn with 600 kernels each and you plant all 1200 kernels. In about seventy-five more days, you will have 1200 stalks with one or two ears each, producing 1,440,000 kernels. This is the law of multiplication.

There is nothing mystical or magical about this. If you sow, you reap. If you sow sparingly, you reap sparingly. If you sow bountifully, you reap bountifully. Having God's perspective and realizing that what you're doing is planting seeds that will result in abundance and increase will make you excited to give.

We are not just talking about crops here. The principle applies to every area of life. What does Luke 6:38 say? "Give, and it will be given to you: good measure, pressed down, shaken together, and running over will be put into your bosom. For with the same measure that you use, it will be measured back to you." I love to be able to give, to plant seeds in other people's lives, fully expecting to see things change and ministries flourish. But the principle of multiplication and sowing and reaping promises that whatever I give, following God's direction, will be poured back, running over, into my life as well.

Have you considered all the areas where you could potentially sow? What about love or forgiveness, patience, mercy, understanding, kindness? This law of multiplication is built into everything that touches us. We don't have time to talk about all the possible places where we can sow life and hope and love with a deep expectation of receiving those things back in "full measure, pressed down, shaken together and running over." It's a beautiful picture of someone with a burlap sack, having seed filled to the top and then taking that sack, shaking it, pressing it down, and filling it more until it overflows.

The preceding verse, Luke 6:37, in the same context says, "Judge not, and you shall not be judged. Condemn not, and you shall not be condemned. Forgive, and you will be forgiven." This universal principle applies toward the sowing of negative things, too—sowing discord, hatred, unforgiveness, or impatience. Why is this so important to understand?

Because YOU determine the harvest!

The principle of sowing involves selection. We choose what kind of seed we want to eventually reap, whether seed in accordance with faith and life in Christ, or in accordance with the flesh and corruption. Do you realize that whatever you need, if you will start giving that very thing, it will start to be measured back to you? Did you catch that? I've had people say, "Well, I need more love." My response is, "Then why don't you begin to extend love to others. Or forgiveness. Or . . ." When will that occur? When will you start to see a return on your seed? I do not know. Some crops take longer to come to fruition.

"You determine the harvest!"

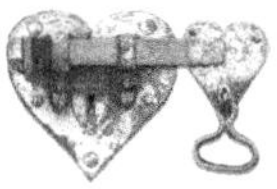

The most important point of this principle is that you sow, recognizing that the Kingdom of God and His righteousness will come to you as you do. In Matthew 6:33, Jesus proclaims, "Seek first the Kingdom of God and His righteousness." He is saying that this is unlike any other kingdom you know. This is Christ's Kingdom under His rule, reign, and dominion. Colossians says that we have been transferred out of and delivered from the kingdom of darkness into the Kingdom of His beloved Son.

Divine Alignment

In the transition from the old kingdom ways of doing things, the structure and beliefs of the new must start with coming under the authority of the Lord, Jesus, and aligning yourself with His principles, having your mind renewed and your thoughts sanctified. This process is accomplished through discipleship. It is a growth process, not unlike the maturation of a seed. In Genesis 1:11, God said that the earth should bring forth grass and herbs that yield seed, and the fruit tree that yields fruit according to its kind whose seed is in itself. And then God said, "Let the earth bring forth living creatures, according to its kind, cattle and creeping things and beasts of the earth, each according to its kind, and so it was" (Genesis 1:24). From the beginning of time, God set into place the principle of seed reproduction, after its own kind, and that is still operating today. "While the earth remains, seedtime and harvest, cold and heat, winter and summer, and day and night shall not cease" (Genesis 8:22). Yes, as long as the earth remains. And the last time I checked, the earth was still here!

In speaking about seed, look with me in Genesis 3:15. "And I will put enmity between you and the woman, and between your seed and her Seed; He shall bruise your head, and you shall bruise His heel." Note the seed is singular, not plural. In Genesis 22:17-18 note this powerful Scripture: "Blessing I will bless you, and multiplying I will multiply your descendants as the stars of the heaven and as the sand which is on the seashore; and your descendants shall possess the gate of their enemies. In your seed all the nations of the earth shall be blessed, because you have obeyed My voice."

God the Father wants to bless His children. He blessed Abram and told him that because he obeyed Him, He was going to multiply Abram's descendants. That use of the word was singular; God did not say "seeds." Galatians 3:16 and 26-29 says,

> Now to Abraham and his Seed were the promises made. He does not say, "And to seeds," as of many, but as of one, "And to your Seed," who is Christ . . . For you are all sons of God through faith in Christ Jesus. For as many of you as were baptized into Christ have put on Christ. There is neither Jew nor Greek, there is neither slave nor free, there is neither male nor female; for you are all one in Christ Jesus. And if you are Christ's, then you are Abraham's seed, and heirs according to the promise.

These Scriptures have nothing to do with money or tithing; however, it's vital that we understand the principle of sowing seeds. Consider what we are dealing with in this nation right now—the racism, division, violence, and disrespect. There is so much hatred and animosity toward each other. These are seeds that are being sown. Do you realize that when it comes to division, that there are only two people groups on the face of the earth? Those in Christ and those not in Christ. It doesn't matter what race you belong to or the color of your skin, whether you are Jew or Greek, slave or free, male or female. The real question is: Are you in Christ or not?

There is no possible way to have unity apart from Christ. We can't fix the devastation on our own. It is only through Him that the world will be reconciled and we will learn to love one another. Galatians 6:7-8 makes it clear. "Do not be deceived, God is not mocked; for whatever a man sows, that he will also reap. For he who sows to his flesh will of the flesh reap corruption, but he who sows to the Spirit will of the Spirit reap everlasting life."

The Apostle Paul says, do not be deceived. How can we be deceived? By thinking that what we sow won't sprout up and produce after its kind. That's deception. If you sow something bad, why would you be shocked that it would produce something bad? That seed is going to produce—and that is the problem, if you're not sowing good seeds.

You may be asking yourself right now the question I've been asked hundreds of times. "Well, if you are giving money in order to just get money back, then that's the wrong idea, isn't it?" No, because I am agreeing with the principle of the Kingdom of God that says whatever you sow you shall reap. It is not that you are giving to get, but if you are NOT sowing financial resources in some form or fashion, how would you expect a crop of money or provision to show up? If you sow cotton, you get cotton; if you sow corn, you get corn. If you sow from your resources or bank account, you can expect to get that in return. It's a universal principle. Are you expecting God to open the windows of Heaven to pour out a blessing upon you (Malachi 3:10)? He wants to, but He is asking that you position your mind, will, and heart in agreement with Him and trust Him. How? By giving, by sowing, and by coming into alignment with His Word and His plan for the resources He has entrusted you with.

> ***"If you sow from your resources or bank account, wouldn't you expect to get that in return?"***

Let me encourage you in this one area. If you have sown bad seeds and are carrying regret or have seen bad fruit begin to come up in your field, then PRAY. Ask God for a crop failure! Take some time to humble yourself and repent for the choices and the places where you have sinned or erred, knowing that He doesn't want any bad seeds to come to fruition. Then commit your ways to sowing with a view toward righteousness and life.

Proving God's Principles

I want to share a couple of personal examples of the blessings of God upon a woman who never wavered in her heart toward giving and sowing, even sacrificially—my mother.

When I was thirteen, we moved off the farm and into the big city of Corsicana. Mom continued to live in that house for forty years, until we moved her to Dallas in 2002. However, in all that time, the air conditioner never had to be repaired! Have you ever heard of an A/C that made it forty years? She had a clothes dryer that never broke down and lasted all those years. Mom was faithful in her giving and tithing and God was faithful to care for her.

Sometimes we get fixated on the money aspect, but there are so many other areas and needs in which God wants to demonstrate His abundant provision. I was doing my own taxes for years. And when I say I did my own taxes, let me rephrase that. I had an accounting firm to do my taxes, but I would fill out all my line items and hand it in to them. I was in the oil and gas business and would drive 50,000 to 60,000 miles a year. I drove a Suburban at the time; in fact, I had several Suburbans. And I have had to repair everything that could be repaired on those many times. So one year, I turned in the list of items on the repairs and maintenance without including gasoline. The previous year, it had totaled $6,000, but that year it was only $60. I thought, well, I know why that is. We had just started using credit cards. I thought, I'll bet I have all those receipts somewhere together, so I'll go look. As I started to search, the Lord spoke to me and said, "Is it easier for Me to keep your car fixed or for Me to give you the money to repair it?" I said, "I'll take 'keep the car fixed!'"

The God of creation has ways that are not our ways and not limited to this finite world. But it takes faith to operate in God's economy, faith to trust Him. "Without faith, it's impossible to please Him, for he who comes to God must believe that He is, and that He is a rewarder of those who diligently seek Him" (Hebrews 11:6). He gives us richly all things to enjoy, but He expects us to steward those things, and "He who is faithful in what is least is faithful also in much; and he who is unjust in what is least is unjust also in much. Therefore if you have not been faithful in the unrighteous mammon, who will commit to your trust the true riches?" (Luke 16:10-11).

Giving finances is attached to growing faith and dependency upon God. I know the mental gymnastics you are going through regarding this huge step of faith. I've been through it myself, looking at my bank account and saying, "There just isn't enough money." But God is saying that you have to start where you are. Things are not going to change until you begin cooperating, agree with God, and take action.

Honestly, this is not a transactional relationship. We don't have financial leverage over the One who made the universe. Giving, likewise, isn't an insurance policy to make all our problems go away. To be clear, God doesn't owe you or me anything just because we give money back to Him. Rather, giving is a response to God's goodness that we've already experienced—and a reminder that He is our hope and future, not the size of our savings account.

I want to direct us to Matthew 25:14-28. This is the parable of the talents. "For the kingdom of heaven is like a man traveling to a far country, who called his own servants and delivered his goods to them. And to one he gave five talents, to another two, and to another one, to each according to his own ability; and immediately he went on a journey."

It's interesting to me that he gave the servants talents according to their ability. We know that not everyone has the same abilities. Not everyone is equal in skill or talent. For example, look at sports personalities and some of their incredible abilities. What about artists or musicians, engineers or IT people? God made each one of us unique. Yes we have equal access to Him through Christ, but no two of us are alike. In this passage, the key point is the faithfulness to use and invest wisely what they had been given, according to their ability.

The master rewarded the faithful stewards, but to the one he called wicked and lazy, he said, "You knew that I reap where I have not sown, and gather where I have not scattered seed. So you ought to have deposited my money with the bankers, and at my coming I would have received back my own with interest. So take the talent from him, and give it to him who has ten talents."

You might say, "Whoa, that's not fair—just wait a minute!" But the Scripture goes on. "For to everyone who has, more will be given, and he will have abundance; but from him who does not have, even what he has will be taken away." The principles that govern the Kingdom of God are sometimes difficult to understand because we think in human terms and somehow believe that God should act the way we do and think how we think. But His ways are not our ways, and we can be confident, grateful, and at peace in that because He is perfect and we're not.

> ***"His ways are not our ways, and we can be grateful and at peace for that."***

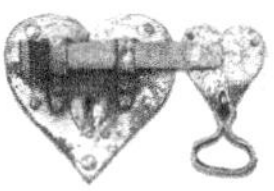

Faithful in Little Things

In Luke 21:1-4, Jesus observes:

> And He looked up and saw the rich putting their gifts into the treasury, and He saw also a certain poor widow putting in two mites. So He said, "Truly I say to you that this poor widow has put in more than all; for all these out of their abundance have put in offerings for God, but she out of her poverty put in all the livelihood that she had."

In this passage, Jesus witnesses this offering of two small copper coins and describes how great this widow's gift is, because it represents a greater proportion of her wealth than the larger gifts of the religious leaders and others. This is an amazing example of a heart that was yielded to God. He put this incredible story in the Bible for us to see and to take notice of the contrast with those who gave out of their abundance. The widow woman gave her all—she didn't have anything left. Jesus wasn't jumping for joy because she had nothing. His heart went out to her. He was publicly revealing the weight that the heart of sacrifice carries.

You may be saying to yourself that you will give more when your next bonus comes in, or when you pay off a few more debts, or next year, or when you get a new job. No, no, no. This is where the grace of giving begins to have a very real impact upon your life. You start with faith. You look at the seed in your hand and you make a determined, prayerful decision to not eat that seed, but instead to sow it, believing that God will bring increase.

Our trust must be in Him; our faith in Him; our focus on living our lives in obedience to His commandments in order that we may be blessed and so that we will be a blessing to others. What does that mean, and how does that look for each of us?

That depends. It is different for everyone. It depends upon your gifts, your talents, your resources, and what the Lord has purposed for your life. Pastor Chris McRae of Sojourn Church has a dynamic gift of preaching and evangelism. What are your gifts and strengths? Do you realize that real success is coming into agreement with who God created you to be? It is saying, "Yes, Lord, I do want to be everything You've desired in Your heart for me to be and do all that You've purposed for me to do." Seek the Lord about His plans for you and how you are to give, serve, and sow into the Kingdom. He has created you as a unique ambassador of His love, placed here on earth to touch lives and be a world changer.

In closing this chapter, I want to share these last few verses from Galatians 6:9-10: "And let us not grow weary while doing good, for in due season we shall reap if we do not lose heart. Therefore, as we have opportunity, let us do good to all, especially to those who are of the household of faith."

Why would God say to not grow weary while doing good? Because we can grow weary, become discouraged, and want to give up! Sometimes the season of waiting for the promise, the harvest, can seem like forever. Indeed, it may be weeks, months, or maybe years. Even in our humanness, the truth is that we take for granted wonderful things. We start out strong, grateful, and appreciative and then grow lukewarm. Paul recognizes this in his letter to Galatia, for he urges his readers to anchor themselves in this truth that "*in due season*" we shall reap. Yes, it may be long. How long? I don't know. But don't lose heart in spending yourself through love, in trusting and believing, persevering, and waiting for the fulfillment of God's promises. He is faithful and He is true to His Word.

♥ TAKE IT TO HEART

The principle of sowing and reaping doesn't discriminate. It applies to believers and non-believers, and it pertains to every area of our lives. We reap what we sow. This may be a new revelation in your understanding of the Kingdom of God, and you are being challenged to consider all the places where you have already sown and wish you hadn't. As I said before, you can always pray for crop failure! God, in His infinite mercy, waits to supply you with good seed and lead you to make changes that will produce a rich, satisfying harvest—life abundant.

Let me encourage you to not lose hope in the waiting, for in due season you WILL reap. Take some time to pray over and pour over the Scriptures in this chapter. Begin today by asking God to give you a new outlook and expectation for the bounty yet to come.

TAKE IT TO GOD

Dear God, I thank You for never growing weary with me. You ceaselessly do good in my life, even though I may not always see or acknowledge it. I ask You to give me the strength and endurance to sow, teach me how to plant the right seeds, and then wait patiently as I pray for increase and multiplication. I ask You to forgive me for my anxious, fearful ways and unbelief about Your love and provision in my life. May my heart be at rest as I learn to give freely and cheerfully by Your Spirit, and may I look for opportunities to bless others and take Your truth and abundance to the world around me. May my life bring glory and honor to You. In Jesus's name. Amen.

CHAPTER SIX

SCRIPTURE REFERENCES

2 Corinthians 9:6-8

Luke 6:38

Genesis 1:11

Genesis 3:15

Genesis 22:17-18

Galatians 3:16, 26-29

Galatians 6:7-10

Luke 16:10-11

Matthew 25:14-28

Luke 21:1-4

Luke 6:37

Matthew 6:33

Genesis 1:24

Genesis 8:22

Malachi 3:10

Hebrews 11:6

Breaking the Spirit of Poverty

John 10:10 reads, "The thief does not come except to steal, and to kill, and to destroy. I have come that they may have life, and that they may have it more abundantly."

This verse captures the scope and sequence of everything that takes place in our lives. You may not realize it, but you have an enemy that wants to kill you, steal your future and your destiny, and destroy your life. He wants to destroy your job, your joy, your happiness, your health, your finances, your marriage, and your kids.

So how does he do that? Through lies. He is a liar, a murderer, the Father of Lies, and a deceiver (John 8:44). And he is on a mission to lie to you. Why, you might ask? Because it's in his nature since the Garden of Eden, when his first lie was delivered to Adam and Eve. He knows that if he can get you to believe a lie, you will be in bondage. Remember, the "truth will make you free." If the truth makes you free, then a lie will hold you captive and will produce unbelief. Unbelief is the absence of faith and without faith, it's impossible to please God. That is the deceiver's ultimate goal—to instill fear and unbelief. His tactic is fear, and he uses this weapon against you because every decision that you make which is based in fear will result in a bad outcome. The thief cannot bear the fact that you possess any kind of blessing. He is unrelenting in his strategies to bring death and destruction to every aspect of your life.

But take note of the promise contained in this verse. Jesus says that He came to give life, and more abundantly! The words "they may have" come from the Greek tense that means "to have and to continually possess." This life that Jesus offers us is *zoe*, which depicts a life that is filled with the power of enduring vitality. What is so beautiful in this verse is that "abundantly" in Greek is the word *periossos* (Strong's Concordance #4053) and it means "to be above, beyond what is regular, extraordinary," or even exceeding.

The Holy Spirit came and indwelt you when you received Jesus Christ as Lord, and it was this abundant life that He gave to you. Truth was woven into your DNA as you were adopted and became God's son or daughter. That exchange of the Cross brought freedom and truth, which is meant to continually lead you into all truth, to set you free, and to produce faith, love, and life.

Revealing Fears and Our Focus

Let's look at Matthew 6:25-34.

> Therefore I say to you, do not worry about your life, what you will eat or what you will drink; nor about your body, what you will put on. Is not life more than food and the body more than clothing? Look at the birds of the air, for they neither sow nor reap nor gather into barns; yet your heavenly Father feeds them. Are you not of more value than they? Which of you by worrying can add one cubit to his stature?
>
> So why do you worry about clothing? Consider the lilies of the field, how they grow: they neither toil nor spin; and yet I say to you that even Solomon in all his glory was not arrayed like one of these. Now if God so clothes the grass of the field, which today is, and tomorrow is thrown into the oven, will He not much more clothe you, O you of little faith?

> Therefore do not worry, saying, "What shall we eat?" or "What shall we drink?" or "What shall we wear?" For after all these things the Gentiles seek. For your heavenly Father knows that you need all these things. But seek first the kingdom of God and His righteousness, and all these things shall be added to you. Therefore do not worry about tomorrow, for tomorrow will worry about its own things. Sufficient for the day is its own trouble.

In this passage, Jesus says, "Remember, we talked about this—don't store up treasures on earth, but store up treasures in Heaven, for wherever your treasure is, there your heart will be." It's not the heart that leads first; it's the treasure; the focus of the eyes.

"It's not the heart that leads first; it's the focus of the eyes."

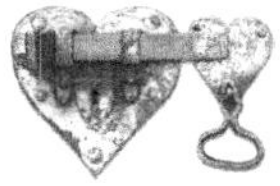

So, what is your focus? We are humans, living in a natural world. We were designed to crave security, love, and affection. But because of this, we often direct this drive in the wrong direction. Have you taken the time to stop and reflect upon your motives and the areas where you invest most of your resources, energy, talents, and time? Many work crazy hours in an attempt to accumulate wealth or build financial security. Others are looking for relationships to fulfill their deepest longings. Or success to satisfy the soul.

In the middle of these verses, Jesus drops in the issue of fear. Why? Because fear is the thief that keeps us from truly experiencing the fullness of all that God has planned for His people and created us to be.

The area of money and finances is an especially challenging one. The enemy comes to steal, kill, and destroy, especially in regard to money. There is a spirit of poverty that we see attached to mammon. Often, it can come through family lines, where there have been misuses or abuses and poverty throughout generations. But we also fall into unbelief and fear about provision that keeps us bound and afraid to give. It stops us from being who God wants us to be. It stifles growth and being a conduit of blessing to others.

You can call it worry. You can call it anxiety or concern. You can even call it frugalness or whatever you want. It has lots of masks, but the root is still fear, and it's important that it be identified and dealt with in order to walk in freedom. Oftentimes, it manifests as control or manipulation, but underlying all of that is fear.

Stewarding Gifts and Abilities

This is an interesting passage in Matthew 25:14-30:

> For the kingdom of heaven is like a man traveling to a far country, who called his own servants and delivered his goods to them. And to one he gave five talents, to another two, and to another one, to each according to his own ability; and immediately he went on a journey. Then he who had received the five talents went and traded with them, and made another five talents. And likewise he who had received two gained two more also. But he who had received one went and dug in the ground, and hid his lord's money. After a long time the lord of those servants came and settled accounts with them.
>
> So he who had received five talents came and brought five other talents, saying, "Lord, you delivered to me five talents; look, I have gained five more talents besides them." His lord said to him, "Well done, good and faithful servant; you were faithful over a few things, I will make you ruler over many things. Enter into the joy of your lord." He also who had received two talents came and said, "Lord, you delivered to me two talents; look, I have gained two more talents besides them."

> His lord said to him, "Well done, good and faithful servant; you have been faithful over a few things, I will make you ruler over many things. Enter into the joy of your lord."
>
> Then he who had received the one talent came and said, "Lord, I knew you to be a hard man, reaping where you have not sown, and gathering where you have not scattered seed. And I was afraid, and went and hid your talent in the ground. Look, there you have what is yours."
>
> But his lord answered and said to him, "You wicked and lazy servant, you knew that I reap where I have not sown, and gather where I have not scattered seed. So you ought to have deposited my money with the bankers, and at my coming I would have received back my own with interest. So take the talent from him, and give it to him who has ten talents."
>
> For to everyone who has, more will be given, and he will have abundance; but from him who does not have, even what he has will be taken away. And cast the unprofitable servant into the outer darkness. There will be weeping and gnashing of teeth.

We looked at this passage in a previous chapter, but it's important to mention it again.

The talents were given to each one *according to his own ability.* God doesn't arbitrarily give expecting you to do something with those resources or gifts, exactly like the next person. We are not all endowed with the same abilities, talents, intelligence, or creativity. Consider sports personalities and their skills and strengths. Most of us could never compete on their level.

Don't make the mistake of thinking you are a five-talent person or a two-talent person. God has created you unique and you are not to compare yourself with another. But the point of this parable is to make it clear that, whatever God has given into your hands, He expects to see increase, stewardship, and a return on His investment. To those who were faithful and managed the resources wisely, the lord gave even more. However, the one who was fearful and hid the money in the ground he called lazy. What he had was taken away, and he was cast into outer darkness.

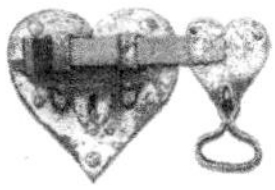

"If fear is operating, it will result in bad decisions."

I don't think I want to end up there; that doesn't sound like a good place! This servant's fear and judgment caused him to make the wrong decision and to lose what he had. Regardless of the choices you will be facing in life, if fear is operating, it is going to result in a bad decision, no matter what it is.

This doesn't just apply to money—it's relative to all areas of life. Understand that it's the enemy's plan to get you to move out and make decisions based upon fear, a wrong view of God or unbelief, and not decisions based in truth or the goodness of a loving God.

We don't know what Heaven will be like or what kind of responsibilities we will have, but this Scripture suggests that there will be rewards for our stewardship and increase connected to our faithfulness. I don't think we will have our big house with a hammock out back where we'll spend our days, swinging in the breeze, drinking mint juleps. But whatever God has planned, He will purposefully invite us to join Him, and perhaps be "ruler over many things," and undoubtedly experience the joy of the Lord.

Wrong Perspectives

In the previous parable, we saw the consequences that the unprofitable servant experienced who had a distorted view of the master, God. In the following story, we will look at the spies who had a wrong concept of themselves and ultimately God's ability to deliver:

> Then they told him, and said: "We went to the land where you sent us. It truly flows with milk and honey, and this is its fruit. Nevertheless the people who dwell in the land are strong; the cities are fortified and very large; moreover we saw the descendants of Anak there. The Amalekites dwell in the land of the South; the Hittites, the Jebusites, and the Amorites dwell in the mountains; and the Canaanites dwell by the sea and along the banks of the Jordan."
>
> Then Caleb quieted the people before Moses, and said, "Let us go up at once and take possession, for we are well able to overcome it." But the men who had gone up with him said, "We are not able to go up against the people, for they are stronger than we." And they gave the children of Israel a bad report of the land which they had spied out, saying, "The land through which we have gone as spies is a land that devours its inhabitants, and all the people whom we saw in it are men of great stature. There we saw the giants (the descendants of Anak came from the giants); and we were like grasshoppers in our own sight, and so we were in their sight." –Numbers 13:27-33

Take some time to read the entire chapter of Numbers 13. You'll realize that God told Moses to "choose leaders out of every tribe." These were not just random men; they were strong leaders, perhaps seasoned warriors, who were chosen to spy out the land of Canaan. God had already told Moses that He was going to give the land to the children of Israel.

So the spies returned with a bad report about the inhabitants, their fortified cities, their numbers, and the giants in the land. Their assessment was, "we were like grasshoppers in our own sight." The spies' view of themselves was wrong. And this is what poverty, and the spirit of poverty, does to a person's perspective.

A poverty mentality distorts and presents a false view of reality. It locks you unto unbelief and produces a twisted, inaccurate perception of everything. It lies to you, saying, "I can't ever get ahead," "I will never be able to get out of debt," "I can't tithe," "I have no money," "I'm broke," "We will end up on the streets," and on and on it goes. Poverty is a thief! It's a belief that the enemy tries to put upon us that is rooted in two things—a wrong view of God and a wrong view of ourselves.

King David had some weak moments and failures, but when facing Goliath, he had no doubt in the greatness of God and His ability to deliver into his hands. Conversely, Saul and his warriors looked at the giant standing ten feet tall with a huge club and thought, "No way; are you kidding me, David? You think you can take this guy out?" But David looked at the uncircumcised Philistine and confidently announced:

> You come to me with a sword, with a spear, and with a javelin. But I come to you in the name of the LORD of hosts, the God of the armies of Israel, whom you have defied. This day the LORD will deliver you into my hand, and I will strike you and take your head from you. And this day I will give the carcasses of the camp of the Philistines to the birds of the air and the wild beasts of the earth, that all the earth may know that there is a God in Israel. Then all this assembly shall know that the LORD does not save with sword and spear; for the battle is the LORD's, and He will give you into our hands. –1 Samuel 17:45-47

David didn't look at the natural, as we so often do, and forget how big our God is. It didn't matter to him if Goliath was forty feet tall or four. All he knew was that this Philistine was not in covenant with the living God. Our challenge is that we get a right perspective about who God is and who we are in Him—children of a covenant-keeping Lord whose goodness is from everlasting to everlasting.

Stronghold of Poverty

There is another aspect of this subject that needs to be recognized and addressed, and it is a stronghold of poverty. 2 Corinthians 10:3-5 says, "For though we walk in the flesh, we do not war according to the flesh. For the weapons of our warfare are not carnal but mighty in God for pulling down strongholds, casting down arguments and every high thing that exalts itself against the knowledge of God, bringing every thought into captivity to the obedience of Christ."

A stronghold of poverty is a mindset. It's a pattern of thinking that is contrary to God's Word. The main characteristic of any stronghold is that it is something you don't believe can ever change. When it comes to poverty, you believe that you'll never get out of that state. It may have come through generational lines. Your family may have always struggled with money or been poor. At some point, you may have just accepted the belief that that is your fate in life as well. It may be rooted in some degree of truth and certainly what you experienced. But according to God's Word, that's not reality. It's a lie from the pit of Hell, and it has to be torn down! It must be destroyed.

"The weapons of our warfare are . . . mighty in God." What are those weapons? Truth. Worship. Thanksgiving. The truth will make you FREE! And it will keep you free. It's the power of God that produces faith, hope, and love.

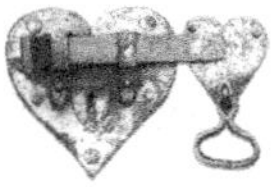

"What are strongholds? Lies, fears, mental blocks."

"[F]or pulling down strongholds." What are strongholds? Lies. Fears. Mental blocks. The Word is clear that you are given dominion over every lie, every argument, all unbelief, and any stronghold that has assaulted you and plagued your family—even for generations!

"[For] casting down arguments." What are the arguments? More lies. More unbelief. Let's make a list:

- † "My family has always had financial issues."
- † "I can never save money."
- † "I'm always broke."
- † "I'll never get out of debt."

"[A]nd every high thing." What are the high things? These are the areas where the enemy accuses God. Vain imaginations such as "God doesn't love you." "Other people are more important to Him than you." "Look what you've done; God isn't going to answer your prayers." They're all lies rooted in fear, and it's time to get free from the deception and the control of the enemy who is attempting to dictate what happens in our lives.

In 2 Timothy 1:7, Paul's words are delivered to Timothy to encourage him, in a world full of challenges, trials, and uncertainty, to remember that there is a God who has given us the power to not only face those challenges, but also to overcome them. "For God has not given us a spirit of fear, but of power and of love and of a sound mind." Yes, there is a spirit of fear operating in the earth realm, but we are exhorted that "There is no fear in love; but perfect love casts out fear, because fear involves torment. But he who fears has not been made perfect in love" (1 John 4:18). The tormentor has been defeated through Christ who came to give LIFE abundantly!

But we also have a choice. Yes, the works of the enemy are evident: lies, thievery, destruction, murder, slander, accusations, fear, and the list goes on. It's interesting that in the Garden of Eden there were two trees. The Tree of Life and the Tree of the Knowledge of Good and Evil. The two trees represent the dichotomy of belief: the tree of the knowledge of good and evil is the law of sin and ultimately death; the tree of life is eternal life and ultimately grace. This is where we see God's first intention toward us. We are able to choose the terms on which we will interact with God. We can choose to obey Him or disobey Him. We can choose to trust Him or not trust Him. The two trees represent this choice.

The admonition in Deuteronomy 30:19-20 is clear—choose LIFE!

> I call heaven and earth as witnesses today against you, that I have set before you life and death, blessing and cursing; therefore choose life, that both you and your descendants may live; that you may love the LORD your God, that you may obey His voice, and that you may cling to Him, for He is your life and the length of your days; and that you may dwell in the land which the LORD swore to your fathers, to Abraham, Isaac, and Jacob, to give them.

What God is saying here is that if you don't choose life, your default is death. Ultimately, by not choosing life, you are choosing death. When your life began, you were dead in your trespasses and sin; however, when you were born again, you became a new creation, given eternal life and the freedom to choose.

Depending on how long you've lived on this earth, you have been making choices—walking in truth or error, choosing life or death, or just being influenced by the world and the culture in which you live.

Truthfully, you probably have a lot of unlearning and untraining to do.

This is why discipleship is so important for growth and maturity. It's in the discipline and accountability while making small sacrifices and better choices that lead to a better life. It creates habits, habits build routines, and routines become who you are daily. The end goal, of course, is that we become more like Christ. We become conformed to His image and represent Him to the world around us.

TAKE IT TO HEART

Contained within the pages of this chapter were weighty, and maybe new to you, truths about the nature and realm of strongholds, fears, and wrong perspectives. Exposing the lies of the enemy is the beginning of freedom in your mindset, beliefs about poverty, and breaking the chains and patterns of failure and lack.

God wants His people free and the Kingdom to expand and advance through believers—through you. Consider grabbing a piece of paper or a journal and recording all the areas in which you believe there has been a spirit of poverty operating. Bring this before the Lord and pray! "Therefore if the Son makes you free, you shall be free indeed" (John 8:36).

TAKE IT TO GOD

Dear God, I pray that You would break me and my family of this spirit of poverty that has plagued us for generations and the destructive mindsets that have held us captive. I ask You to forgive me for living my life based upon these lies and fears about money and resources that have allowed the enemy to steal, kill, and destroy. Show me the areas of my unbelief and set me free.

Lord, fill me with Your perfect love so that my heart fully trusts in You, and close the door to this stronghold. I give You, Holy Spirit, permission to excavate, to search out my ways, and bring me to a place of healing, hope, and prosperity—body, soul, and spirit. Show me the real definition of prosperity. You have set before me life and death. I choose LIFE—today and always. In Jesus's name. Amen.

CHAPTER SEVEN

SCRIPTURE REFERENCES

John 10:10

Matthew 6:25-34

Matthew 25:14-30

Numbers 13:27-33

1 Samuel 17:45-47

2 Corinthians 10:3-5

2 Timothy 1:7

1 John 4:18

Deuteronomy 30:19-20

John 8:36

John 8:44

8

Created for Good Works

For we are His workmanship, created in Christ Jesus for good works, which God prepared beforehand that we should walk in them.

Ephesians 2:10

The Apostle Paul wrote to the church in Ephesus, who were followers of Jesus Christ, these words to exhort them to stand strong and to remain faithful to their calling. God has given to us all the instructions that we need to exercise faith and live out what He has called us to do. Work is one of those areas.

In Matthew 5:14-16, Jesus said, "You are the light of the world. A city that is set on a hill cannot be hidden. Nor do they light a lamp and put it under a basket, but on a lampstand, and it gives light to all who are in the house. Let your light so shine before men, that they may see your good works and glorify your Father in heaven."

In both of these Scriptures, the term good works is used. What are good works? Good works are works that are done for God's glory. They are good because they honor God and love people. They are done for God's glory, by God's strength, because God commands. This is not talking about working, but I want to spin off this because the fact of the matter is that God has created us to work. That is what John 5:17 says when Jesus answered the Jews who sought to persecute Him and said, "My Father has been working until now and I've been working."

So evidently God works! Jesus works. Interesting. As a people, we have needed to recognize that work is not something evil to avoid. Work is holy. Actually, work is an expression of worship. We were created to work. Let's look at Genesis 2:1-3. "Thus the heavens and the earth, and all the host of them, were finished. And on the seventh day God ended His work which He had done, and He rested on the seventh day from all His work which He had done. Then God blessed the seventh day and sanctified it, because in it He rested from all His work which God had created and made." God is a creator, and He created work.

God's plan from the beginning of time was for man to work as well. Genesis 2:15 reads,

> "Then the Lord God took the man and put him in the garden of Eden to tend and keep it." And 1 Corinthians 3:9 says, "For we are God's fellow workers; you are God's field, you are God's building." Another Scripture referencing our work is found in Colossians 3:23-24. "And whatever you do, do it heartily, as to the Lord and not to men, knowing that from the Lord you will receive the reward of the inheritance; for you serve the Lord Christ."

Some people may say that work is evil because of the curse that came through Adam and Eve (Genesis 3:17-19). However, the fact is that God hasn't changed His mind about work. "For even when we were with you, we commanded you this: If anyone will not work, neither shall he eat. For we hear that there are some who walk among you in a disorderly manner, not working at all, but are busybodies. Now those who are such we command and exhort through our Lord Jesus Christ that they work in quietness and eat their own bread" (2 Thessalonians 3:10-12). It is something that He created us to do. Why? Because that is where we have the opportunity to display His nature and the expression of who He is. His workmanship demonstrates the greatness and the goodness of the loving Creator.

Attitudes and Ethics

What kind of attitude and work ethic are you reflecting in the workplace? I might be a pretty good Christian on Sunday, but what about on Monday and Tuesday and Wednesday, and so on? I think we should be the best employees ever. We should be the last person that a company would let go because we make such a huge difference in their business. I'm not saying that you should be a workaholic or a man-pleaser. No, but we are to work heartily, diligently, honestly, efficiently as unto the Lord.

We should be atmosphere changers, able to shift the workplace environment to something positive if it has been negative. We carry the presence of God and can invite Him to come and bring peace. If I am in Him, then everywhere I go, I carry an aroma of Christ.

"We should be atmosphere changers... because we carry the presence of God."

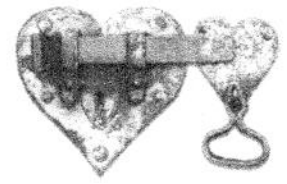

We have been given dominion over the earth to work and manage it, and God asks that we cooperate with Him in every sphere of influence. The workplace is a vitally important arena for us to serve His purposes, give ourselves away, exercise the authority of His Kingdom, and be salt and light.

Many years ago, we had a young woman who came to work for the church in an administrative position who had spent five years in a federal prison. She came to know Christ while in prison, and, boy, you talk about a tough place to be salt and light! She had no place that was private or quiet just to herself to pray or read, except her bunk and a broom closet. But she would take authority over that small space and declare that it was hers, a blessing, she would be happy, and would invite God's presence into that space. And everywhere she went, she would literally carry the presence of the Lord.

People could sense it. You can make the same difference in the atmosphere by your life, yielded to Him.

Do you realize that the Spirit of God dwells within you, and He is your advantage? That's what the Word says in John 16:7: "Nevertheless I tell you the truth. It is to your advantage that I go away; for if I do not go away, the Helper will not come to you; but if I depart, I will send Him to you."

We have an advantage over other people who are not believers. Why? Because the Spirit of God who searches all things, reveals truth, leads us, and teaches us actually makes known to us the things that are given to us by God. This Spirit indwells you and me. Through Him we learn how to pursue and cultivate intimacy and an understanding of spiritual things. Then we can discern the things going on around us, be a conduit of His love, and bring transformation wherever we go.

I'm not talking about putting Jesus stickers on the water cooler at work. I'm talking about living in such a manner that men and women see your good works and experience a hunger and thirst for God. They sense that there's something different about your life. They acknowledge that there is a Father in Heaven and long to know Him.

You have the privilege of getting to go to work. Yes, the opportunity to express the very nature and character of Christ in the marketplace, the classroom, the clinic, the retail store, or the carwash. It may not be very exciting or rewarding or where you want to stay, but you don't know whom you'll come in contact with who needs healing or hope or Jesus. In that moment, you are God's ambassador, His servant, carrying the very presence of Almighty God to bring life to someone in need. We are all called to be servants and express the nature of God in work. If you want to be great in God's Kingdom, be a servant.

Taking Action

Proverbs 6:6-11 says:

> Go to the ant, you sluggard!
>
> Consider her ways and be wise,
>
> Which, having no captain,
>
> Overseer or ruler,
>
> Provides her supplies in the summer,
>
> And gathers her food in the harvest.
>
> How long will you slumber, O sluggard?
>
> When will you rise from your sleep?
>
> A little sleep, a little slumber,
>
> A little folding of the hands to sleep—
>
> So shall your poverty come on you like a prowler,
>
> And your need like an armed man.

The book of Proverbs is full of Scriptures which talk about the lazy, the slothful, and the sluggard, and compare them with those who work hard. Notice this chapter of Proverbs 24, verses 30-34:

> I went by the field of the lazy man,
>
> And by the vineyard of the man devoid of understanding;
>
> And there it was, all overgrown with thorns;
>
> Its surface was covered with nettles;

Its stone wall was broken down.

When I saw it, I considered it well;

I looked on it and received instruction:

A little sleep, a little slumber,

A little folding of the hands to rest;

So shall your poverty come like a prowler,

And your need like an armed man.

How many of us don't realize that there are resources within us that we have yet to tap into and explore? We may have settled into unbelief or disbelief and convinced ourselves that we lack even basic qualities or gifts and strengths to succeed. This is a critical area where we need to come into agreement and alignment with who God says we are.

"There are resources within us that we have yet to tap into and explore."

Once you acknowledge that God created you, that you're not a mistake, that He is a good Father and has only good in store for you, then you will begin to see the hard, dry, fallow ground in your thinking, and heart, begin to break up. The key is in the revealing of those things and in the movement.

I grew up on a farm in Texas in the days when we had no power steering on any vehicles. It's nearly impossible to steer a car or turn the steering wheel until you get the car moving. You have to get moving. Begin to explore and find out what the right way is for you to go.

I never had any intention of becoming a pastor. Susan and I never considered that at all. But we were moving and listening to God.

Did we have questions and concerns? Absolutely. But we just kept moving forward, and God continued to reveal things, open doors, and confirm His leading. It didn't matter what we hadn't done, could have done, should have done. What mattered is that we knew God was the same, yesterday, today, and forever, and that all of our tomorrows are good in Him.

Don't allow fear or negative beliefs to cloud your judgment or block your hearing. Proverbs 26:13 talks about the lazy man who says,

> There is a lion in the road!
>
> A fierce lion is in the streets!
>
> As a door turns on its hinges,
>
> So does the lazy man on his bed.
>
> The lazy man buries his hand in the bowl;
>
> It wearies him to bring it back to his mouth.
>
> The lazy man is wiser in his own eyes
>
> Than seven men who can answer sensibly.

The writer of Proverbs is saying there is always a problem or an excuse. Always. There is always a lion roaring outside your door, threatening you and lying to you. There's always something—an obstacle—some reason why things are not going to work out or will fail. Stand against that voice, that lion, that fear, and tell it that you're NOT going to allow it to steal from you any longer!

Unto the Lord

Colossians 3:22 – 4:1 says:

> Bondservants, obey in all things your masters according to the flesh, not with eyeservice, as men-pleasers, but in sincerity of heart, fearing God. And whatever you do, do it heartily, as to the Lord and not to men, knowing that from the Lord you will receive the reward of the inheritance; for you serve the Lord Christ. But he who does wrong will be repaid for what he has done, and there is no partiality.
>
> Masters, give your bondservants what is just and fair, knowing that you also have a Master in heaven.

What this passage is saying is, don't just work so that others can see what you're doing and recognize your work, or only when the boss is around so you'll get accolades. We are to work unto God, with joy, heartily, and as a result, our service will be pleasing to whomever we work for. Our life becomes a fragrance of God to the world as we express His very nature in our dedication and commitment to our Master. His standard is far above that of man, and so are His blessings.

Whether you are in the marketplace, at home, in your neighborhood, at your school, in a government office, or at the supermarket, these are the places where we are to be faithfully serving—not unto man, but unto God, knowing that it is from the Lord that we will receive His just reward. Work is our sacrifice of worship, and He calls it holy.

Getting Practical

In order to make significant life-changes in the area of finances, you have to have a plan. That plan is called a BUDGET! Everyone needs a budget. I don't know of any business that doesn't operate on a budget.

The church of which I am the founding pastor has a budget. We have a plan to handle God's money and demonstrate accountability, fiscal responsibility, and stewardship for the funds that are entrusted to us.

It's no different for a family or a ministry, however large or small. And in order to get out of debt, you have to have a plan for that as well. As we've talked about in previous chapters, consumer debt will kill you. The Word is clear that we are to "owe no man anything" but love and the "borrower is a slave to the lender." It's the scheme of the enemy to keep God's people in bondage. We make purchases for things we cannot afford and then we have to pay that back with high interest rates.

"In order to get out of debt, you have to have a plan."

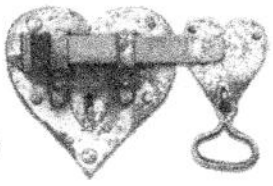

Begin by setting up a simple budget (see Appendix). Start with your gross monthly income, less your tithe. You may want to add in giving, and then obviously your taxes. Savings should be budgeted as well; 15 percent is recommended. On the sheet, you'll see other categories that will help you identify your monthly expenditures, such as rent, food, gas, transportation, electricity, medical insurance, etc. There are hundreds of programs, books, and guides online to assist you in setting up a workable budget.

Let me encourage you to consider taking the Dave Ramsey course. These classes have been invaluable to our church community as we have periodically offered the program. Don't wait or put off doing whatever you need to do to get out of debt and get on a pathway to financial freedom. Begin by tithing and watch God do amazing things with your finances.

As hard as it may be to consider, you may need to get a second or third job for a season. We had a banker friend a few years ago who was a part of our church. He had a late meeting and stopped into a 7-11. Lee walked up to the cash register to pay and recognized the cashier. The gentleman said, "I know what you're thinking—what am I doing here working at night?" The cashier, an Asian man, worked at the same bank with Lee during the day. He continued, "Americans are all about their jobs, their positions, but to me, it's the honor of paying my bills. I've gotten myself into some problems and I'm going to do whatever it takes to get myself out of debt." Needless to say, that made quite an impression on Lee. It's that kind of determination that will change your financial condition. The testimonies of breakthrough and freedom have been worth the hardship.

Is it easy? No, it's not. And it takes time, months or even years. For me personally, it took eight years. It may require you making a lot of sacrifices or keeping money in envelopes so you'll know what you're spending. But God is committed to your freedom and will empower you to walk it out. Our loving Father wants you to have the blessings of His provision that He promised to Abraham and for all of humanity. He doesn't want the enemy to have any control over you, your finances, or any area of your life. You were created to be a conduit for Kingdom resources through whom He might display His splendor, His majesty, and His goodness. Take Him at His Word; test Him, and see Him pour out blessings that you cannot contain! "For the eyes of the LORD run to and fro throughout the whole earth, to show Himself strong on behalf of those whose heart is loyal to Him" (2 Chronicles 16:9). So be it!

TAKE IT TO GOD

Dear God, You know my heart is heavy with the weight of responsibilities I carry and the burden of an awareness of your Divine order and the stewardship You have entrusted to me. Please forgive me for the decisions that I have made which have cost me dearly and not led to freedom and hope. Turn my eyes and my heart toward serving You with the resources You have provided and to understand that I was created for good works that I should walk in them.

Help me to honor You in my work and reflect a grateful heart in all that I do, whether at home, in my community, or in the marketplace. Let my life bring glory to You. In Jesus's name. Amen.

CHAPTER EIGHT

SCRIPTURE REFERENCES

Ephesians 2:10

Matthew 5:14-16

John 5:17

Genesis 2:1-3

Genesis 2:15

Genesis 3:17-19

2 Thessalonians 3:10-12

John 16:7

Proverbs 24:30-34

Proverbs 26:13

Colossians 3:22 – 4:1

1 Corinthinas 3:9

Proverbs 6:6-11

2 Chronicles 16:9

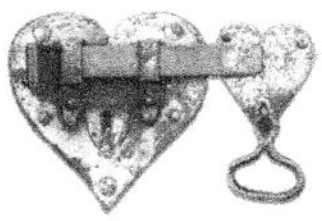

APPENDIX:
PERSONAL MONTHLY BUDGET

Below is a sample budget from Ramsey Solutions.
For more information on budgeting, visit www.ramseysolutions.com.

ZERO-BASED BUDGET

With a zero-based budget, you'll give every incoming dollar a job to do so your money's working *for* you.

Yes, this budget form has a lot of lines and blanks.

But that's okay. We do that so we can list practically every expense imaginable on this form to prevent you from forgetting something. Don't expect to put something on every line. Just use the ones that are relevant to your specific situation.

Step 1

Enter your monthly take-home pay in the box at the top right (**A**). This is the amount you have for the month to budget. So far so good, huh?

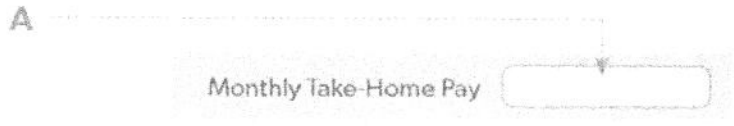

Step 2

Within each main category, such as Food, there are subcategories, like Groceries. Start at the top and work your way down, filling out the Budgeted column (**B**) first. Add up each subcategory and put that number in the Total box (**C**).

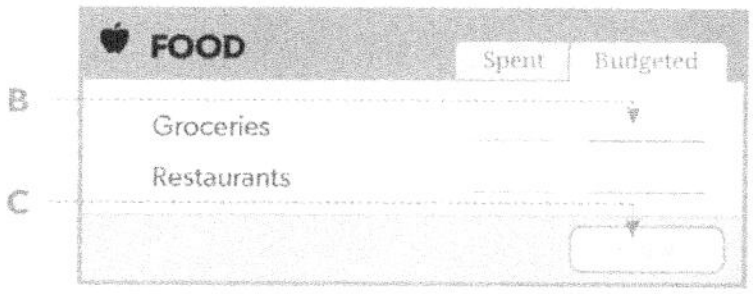

Step 3

Finally, enter your take-home pay in the top box at the end of the page (**D**), then add up all categories and place that total in the Category Totals box (**E**). Then subtract your Category Totals amount from your Take-Home Pay. You should have a zero balance (**F**). Doesn't that feel great?

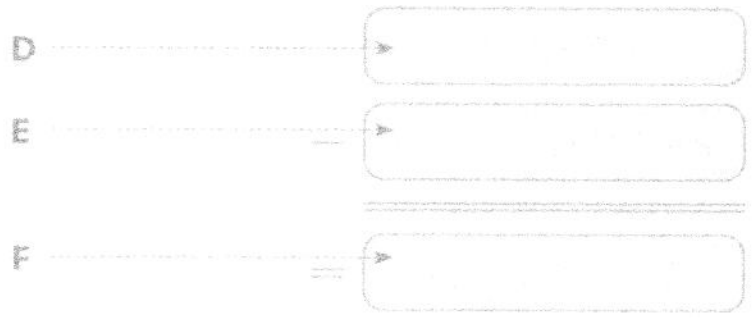

Step 4

When the month ends, put what you actually spent in the Spent column (**G**). That will help you make any necessary adjustments to the next month's budget.

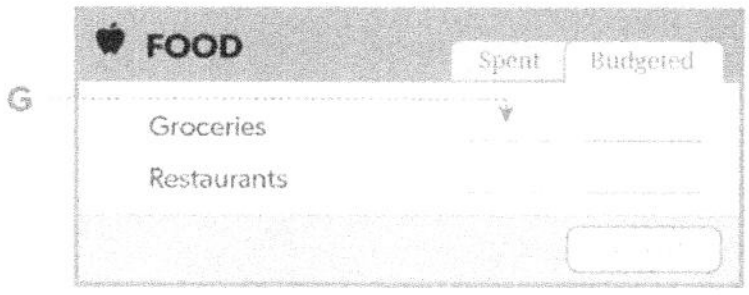

Monthly Take-Home Pay ______

Add up budgeted column & enter here

These icons represent good options for cash envelopes

CHARITY

	Spent	Budgeted
Tithes		
Charity & Offerings		
		TOTAL

SAVING

	Spent	Budgeted
Emergency Fund		
Retirement Fund		
College Fund		
		TOTAL

HOUSING

	Spent	Budgeted
First Mortgage/Rent		
Second Mortgage		
Real Estate Taxes		
Repairs/Maint.		
Association Dues		
		TOTAL

UTILITIES

	Spent	Budgeted
Electricity		
Gas		
Water		
Trash		
Phone/Mobile		
Internet		
Cable		
		TOTAL

FOOD

	Spent	Budgeted
Groceries		
Restaurants		
		TOTAL

CLOTHING

	Spent	Budgeted
Adults		
Children		
Cleaning/Laundry		
		TOTAL

TRANSPORTATION

	Spent	Budgeted
Gas & Oil		
Repairs & Tires		
License & Taxes		
Car Replacement		
Other ______		
		TOTAL

MEDICAL/HEALTH

	Spent	Budgeted
Medications		
Doctor Bills		
Dentist		
Optometrist		
Vitamins		
Other ______		
Other ______		
		TOTAL

INSURANCE

	Spent	Budgeted
Life Insurance		
Health Insurance		
Homeowner/Renter		
Auto Insurance		
Disability Insurance		
Identity Theft		
Long-Term Care		

PERSONAL

	Spent	Budgeted
Child Care/Sitter		
Toiletries		
Cosmetics/Hair Care		
Education/Tuition		
Books/Supplies		
Child Support		
Alimony		
Subscriptions		
Organization Dues		
Gifts (inc. Christmas)		
Replace Furniture		
Pocket Money (His)		
Pocket Money (Hers)		
Baby Supplies		
Pet Supplies		
Music/Technology		
Miscellaneous		
Other ________		
Other ________		

RECREATION

	Spent	Budgeted
Entertainment		
Vacation		

DEBTS

	Spent	Budgeted
Car Payment 1		
Car Payment 2		
Credit Card 1 ________		
Credit Card 2 ________		
Credit Card 3 ________		
Credit Card 4 ________		
Credit Card 5 ________		
Student Loan 1		
Student Loan 2		
Student Loan 3		
Student Loan 4		
Other ________		
Other ________		
Other ________		
Other ________		
Other ________		

Once you have completed filling out each category, subtract all category totals from your take-home pay.

Use the Income Sources form if necessary

Add up totals from each category

Remember — The goal of a zero-based budget is to get this number to zero

ABOUT THE AUTHOR

Terry Moore graduated from SMU with a degree in business administration. After graduating, Terry married his childhood sweetheart, Susan Stroube Moore, who also graduated from SMU's Class of 1973. Shortly thereafter, Terry began his career in commercial real estate and subsequently diversified into the oil & gas industry as an investor and an independent producer.

Terry and Susan became successful business owners, active in their church and community. In 1982, the couple attended a Christian conference where they encountered the Lord in a life-changing way. The Moores then began a Bible Study in their home, which continued for four years and influenced many people who encouraged them to consider starting a church. In January 1987, Terry and Susan, along with several other couples from the Bible Study, founded Sojourn Church. This was a major shift for Terry who had never considered ministry as a career option. Under his leadership, the church continued to grow, resulting in the 1997 relocation to its current facility in Carrollton, Texas. As the membership increased with families from around the Metroplex, the Moores were instrumental in raising up leaders and planting new churches in the region.

For nearly three decades, Sojourn Church has been instrumental in coordinating and hosting conferences for thousands of participants locally and globally. Additionally, Terry and Susan partner with several local inner-city ministries, which feed the poor, offer recovery programs, provide after school programs and adult education for re-entry into mainstream society.

Terry spends much of his time preparing messages, meeting with leaders, and encouraging others. He has written a number of Bible studies designed to equip Christians to live victoriously. He serves on the board of several local ministries, as well as many international organizations.

Terry and Susan have traveled extensively around the world. They continue to be involved in a number of overseas missions where they equip pastors and church leaders with the life-changing power of Jesus Christ.

Terry is the Founding Pastor and an Elder of Sojourn Church. He and Susan have been married forty-seven years and have a son and daughter-in-law who have two teenage children, and daughter and son-in-law who have three young daughters.

MORE TITLES AVAILABLE IN THE ADVANCED FOUNDATIONS SERIES

The Cross is the Key

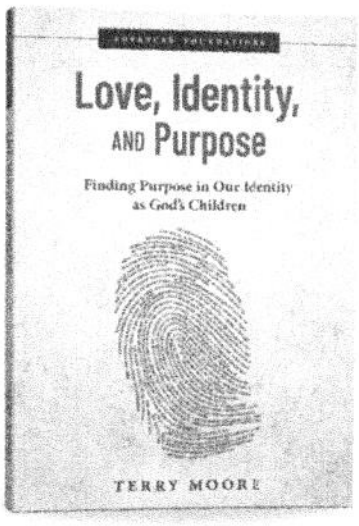

Love, Identity & Purpose

Free Indeed

Hearing God

Basic Training

Setting the Captives Free

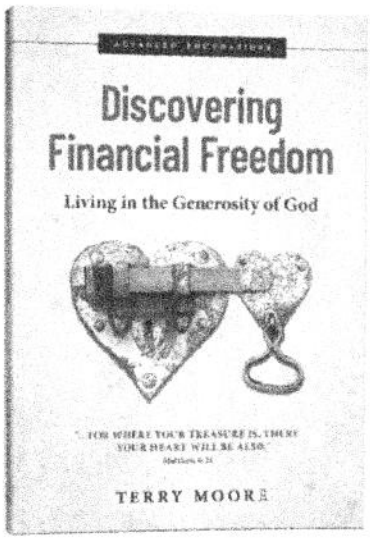

Discovering Financial Freedom

A video series for these titles is available at advancedbiblicalfoundations.org/watch

For more information on titles in this series, please visit: www.advancedbiblicalfoundations.org

Made in the USA
Monee, IL
04 November 2026

67383098R00075